WAYNE PENELLO & ANDREW P. FURMAN

RISK
IS AN
ASSET

TURNING COMMODITY PRICE UNCERTAINTY
INTO A STRATEGIC ADVANTAGE

ForbesBooks

Published by ForbesBooks, Charleston, South Carolina.
Member of Advantage Media Group.

ForbesBooks is a registered trademark, and the ForbesBooks colophon is a trademark of Forbes Media, LLC.

Printed in the United States of America.

10 9 8 7 6 5 4 3 2 1

ISBN: 978-1-95086-302-0
LCCN: 2020906173

Cover design by Carly Blake.
Layout design by Megan Elger.

This publication is designed to provide accurate and authoritative information in regard to the subject matter covered. It is sold with the understanding that the publisher is not engaged in rendering legal, accounting, or other professional services. If legal advice or other expert assistance is required, the services of a competent professional person should be sought.

Advantage Media Group is proud to be a part of the Tree Neutral® program. Tree Neutral offsets the number of trees consumed in the production and printing of this book by taking proactive steps such as planting trees in direct proportion to the number of trees used to print books. To learn more about Tree Neutral, please visit www.treeneutral.com.

Since 1917, the Forbes mission has remained constant. Global Champions of Entrepreneurial Capitalism. ForbesBooks exists to further that aim by bringing the Stories, Passion, and Knowledge of top thought leaders to the forefront. ForbesBooks brings you The Best in Business. To be considered for publication, please visit www.forbesbooks.com.

I dedicate this book to Jim Vaughn, PhD, and my professors at Stony Brook University. Without their inspiration, confidence, and patience, my path would not have been possible.
—WAYNE PENELLO

I dedicate this book to the memory of Harold Lilie, fellow floor trader, stepfather, and the person who taught me my first lesson in risk management—coming back to trade the next day.
—ANDREW FURMAN

CONTENTS

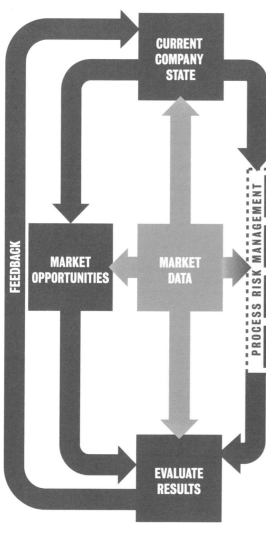

FEEDBACK

CURRENT COMPANY STATE

MARKET OPPORTUNITIES

MARKET DATA

PROCESS RISK MANAGEMENT

EVALUATE RESULTS

PROCESS RISK MANAGEMENT

Using a disciplined, process-based approach to managing your risk will ensure you meet all financial and budgetary targets.

ACKNOWLEDGMENTS

This book would not have been possible without the untold contributions of others we have met and who influenced us throughout our careers. We would like to give special thanks to our clients, who have asked us to develop solutions for them and assist them with the management of their challenges. Many of these provided the spark of inspiration that allowed us to create new perspectives, ideas, and products that we share with you in this book. For two decades, clients have trusted us to help them with strategic decisions that have played an important role in their successes. Additionally, it is with honor that we recognize the team at Risked Revenue Energy Associates (or R^2, pronounced "R squared"). Their talents, efforts, integrity, and creativity have been the foundation for the success that allowed our firm to grow, learn, and innovate. They have dedicated large segments of their careers to us, for which we are most grateful. They are trusted allies and confidants. Without the many contributions of R^2's clients and team, this book would not have been possible.

ABOUT THE AUTHORS

Wayne Penello is the president and founder of Risked Revenue Energy Associates (R^2 or "R squared"). Since 2001, the firm has been developing financial solutions for corporations and private equity firms that wish to enter, optimize, or exit the energy-trading/marketing arena. R^2 currently assists clients with the management of more than $65 billion in assets. In 2010, Mr. Penello was awarded a patent for R^2's methodology for quantifying risk (US Patent 7,822,670 B2). He has forty years of market-making, option-trading, and asset management experience in the energy industry. Mr. Penello began his career on the New York Mercantile Exchange, where he was a market maker and served as ring chairman of options trading.

Subsequently, he held positions managing globally distributed energy assets for Vitol S.A., Vitol U.S.A., Tenneco Gas Marketing, and Torch Energy. Mr. Penello was formerly a research scientist. He holds a master's degree in marine sciences from Stony Brook University and an undergraduate degree in marine biology from Southampton College.

Andrew Furman has thirty-five years of experience in energy and trading. For the past twelve years at R^2, he has delivered hedge solutions to senior management of public corporations, private firms, institutions, and utilities. Prior to joining R^2, Mr. Furman was a managing member of Atlantic Capital Consultants, a member firm on the NYMEX. At Atlantic, he designed the commodity options training and risk-management platform, which launched the careers of many successful professionals in the energy industry. After serving as a managing director at two hedge funds, he assisted in the growth of R^2 through the deployment of its patented analytics. A risk-management and financial-engineering expert, Mr. Furman received a bachelor of science degree in chemical engineering from MIT.

Learning to Manage Uncertainty

Being a Navy SEAL and sniper taught me all about risk management. Take away all the risk variables under your control and reduce it to an acceptable level. The same fundamentals apply in business.

—Brandon Webb, Navy SEAL and best-selling author

LIFE IS FILLED WITH UNCERTAINTY. What will happen cannot be known, but the gap between a possible "good" and "bad" outcome is what is commonly referred to as "risk." Risk is all around us and gives meaning to life. We couldn't exist without it. In reference to the above quote, you don't have to be a Navy SEAL to recognize that risk is present in many of our life's decisions—from choosing a career, to cooking dinner, to falling in love.

Everyone routinely accepts risk into our lives, but rarely do we gamble. Let's take a moment to consider the difference between a gamble and a risk. Each of us confronts gambles and risks regularly, but if we are to avoid poor decisions it is important that we recognize

1

the difference. They can be easily confused because each requires the acceptance of uncertainty. But that is where the similarity ends. Uncertainty that is not managed is a gamble. When uncertainty is managed it becomes a risk. When it is managed with a deliberate process it becomes a calculated risk. Calculated risks are an asset. They do not provide guaranteed returns but are expected to provide a benefit over time. This book explores how using a process to manage uncertainty turns risk into an asset.

Consider that almost every adult in the US drives a car, undeterred by the fact that each year forty thousand people die in car crashes.[1] So why do people drive? Because, despite the obvious risk involved, driving is an asset. It creates opportunity and enhances the quality of our lives. For protection, everyone has car insurance. That covers us financially, but it is not what keeps us safe.

Driving is an asset because, whether we think about it or not, every driver has a process to minimize and manage the risk while on the road. A process enables drivers to adapt their behavior to the specific conditions at hand and to change behaviors when it is appropriate.

Using this premise as a springboard, we have concluded that by using a process, we turn risk into an asset. What do we mean by "a process"? It is a procedure that one uses to check for vulnerabilities and identifies how to respond, repeatedly, over and over again. We can even go a step further and argue that if you fail to monitor risk in a systematic fashion, the best you can hope for is a random outcome. You have not eliminated the possibility of an unwanted result, and at worst you may find yourself in the midst of a disaster.

---

1   "Motor Vehicle Deaths Estimated to Have Dropped 2% in 2019," National Safety Council, accessed February 24, 2020, https://www.nsc.org/road-safety/safety-topics/fatality-estimates.

Who would not properly monitor and manage risk? An even better question is ... *why wouldn't you?*

Welcome to the world of traditional hedging.

We have spent the better part of forty years investigating traditional hedging practices and innovating a better solution; that innovation put us on a path to invent a groundbreaking approach to hedging. Our firm, Risked Revenue Energy Associates (R^2), is a risk-management consultancy that uses a hedge process to transform corporate price risk into a strategic advantage. Since its inception, R^2 has helped to deliver nearly $10 billion to its clients' bottom lines, from PE start-ups to S&P 500 companies. While the past success of R^2 clients is no indication of their future results, the consistency and length of this track record tells us that this approach is making a significant difference. With $65 billion of assets under advisement, our firm provides risk assessments and management strategies on more than two billion barrels of oil equivalent (BOE) per day, which accounts for approximately 10 percent of all oil and gas produced in the United States.

Risk Is an Asset tells the story of innovation, and it will transform the way you think about hedging. What you will learn by reading this book is that effective hedging is not a decision, it is a process. We call this Process Risk Management or PRM. It is guided by risk metrics expressed in the same budgetary terms used to measure the success of your business. PRM helps each firm to maintain focus on its own budgetary success and avoid the trap of trying to outguess the market. Decision makers are kept informed of important developments because PRM tracks and reports in budgetary terms how changes in the marketplace, and/or by management itself, may impact a firm's future performance.

Why is measuring risk in budgetary terms important? Because

if you measure the wrong things, you are unlikely to get the results you want. It is not enough to estimate that fifty-dollar-per-barrel oil could fall to twenty-five dollars or rise to eighty-five dollars. Unless you convert those estimates into budgetary terms, i.e. the metrics used to measure the firm's success, their relevance is not obvious. Let's assume a firm will produce one million barrels of oil. More than likely its budget will be for $50 million in revenue. Assuming the firm has overhead of $40 million, it looks like it will make a handy profit of $10 million. However, if prices fall to twenty-five dollars per barrel the firm's revenues will fall to $25 million, which would be $15 million short of its overhead. Shouldn't the firm have a plan for this possibility? Would twenty-five-dollar oil mean bankruptcy? Could the firm withstand a smaller shock, perhaps to forty dollars per barrel? If the answer is yes, the firm should consider removing $15 million of risk, ensuring that it will generate $40 million in revenue.

The beauty of PRM is that you don't do this once and assume you are safe. No, the world of commodities is dynamic, fast moving, and occasionally treacherous. Begin by getting the firm safe and then employ a process to monitor both your assumptions and market conditions to confirm that it remains safe. That's what this book is about. It was written to identify which metrics are important for you, explain how to risk them and how to manage that risk. Enterprise risk is the sum of all components that can positively and negatively affect a business. PRM is the holistic process of assessment, response, review, and reassessment of commodity price risk.

> Enterprise risk is the sum of all components that can positively and negatively affect a business. PRM is the holistic process of assessment, response, review, and reassessment of commodity price risk.

THE PATH THAT LED TO INNOVATION

How did an oceanographer and a chemical engineer join forces to revolutionize commodity price risk management? We met by chance on the floor of the New York Mercantile Exchange (NYMEX), just when options trading was introduced as a new product. Each of us was drawn to options trading because it allowed us to use our academic backgrounds to an advantage.

Wayne Penello

My journey to the NYMEX began just thirty miles from Wall Street, where I attended Stony Brook University on Long Island. My plan was to become a research scientist. I studied oceanography and developed an appreciation for complex systems like oceans and atmosphere, as well as an expertise in statistics. Statistics proved to be an important tool for me to identify and quantify relationships in the real world. No longer were my views simply opinions—they were grounded in science and useful for predicting events.

Statistics served me well while I was pursuing my advanced degree. I was able to apply my knowledge to filter through data my advisers had abandoned as worthless. My analytical approach allowed me to identify and quantify trends. Working closely with my advisers, I published several professional papers in fields unrelated to oceanography. This was my first successful effort to apply statistics outside of my chosen field of interest.

During my years in graduate school, one quirk of fate led to another, introducing new opportunities for me to explore. One in particular changed my life forever. I had an adviser who required me to read the *New York Times* cover to cover every day. His position was that good scientists were well-read and current. This was in the late 1970s, when home mortgage rates often exceeded 10 percent and savings deposits received in excess of 5 percent interest. One day as I happened to be looking over some commodity-trading data, it suddenly occurred to me that if inflation remained high and I bought gold, I could double my money by the time I graduated. That turned out to be wrong, however. I doubled my money in just four months.

This piqued my curiosity. I was simply fascinated with what the commodity markets were all about. I took advantage of a free three hour class on commodities trading held in New York City once a week. That led to an opportunity for me to visit the trading floor. The place was filled with energy and hummed like a beehive. In contrast, the life of a research scientist I had been living was slow and methodical. Needless to say, I was drawn to the trading floor like a moth to a flame. It wasn't long after that I abandoned my quest to be a research oceanographer and found a position working on the trading floor full time.

Andrew Furman

My route to the trading floor, on the other hand, began with a summer job during high school. It was back in 1979 that my career in commodities was launched from the bottom rung as a runner in the metals markets. Like Wayne, I found it exciting to be on the trading floor. There was so much action, excitement, and drama as the markets ebbed and flowed. Another trait I shared with Wayne was that I also had a passion for science and process. When I graduated high school, I went off to get a chemical engineering degree from MIT. MIT provided me with a great education, but the tremendous lure of being on the trading floor continued to pull at me. Knowing this, my stepfather, Harold Lilie, who was a "local" in platinum and palladium arbitrage, offered me a job to work alongside him. I leaped at the opportunity.

A MODEL IS BORN

Wayne moved to Houston—the energy mecca of the world—in the early 1990s. There he worked with various energy companies in various capacities but always in the role of helping them manage risk or hedge. What Wayne observed was astounding. Whenever hedging came up on the day's agenda, many companies would just do it blindly.

Wayne remembers one CFO in particular who was convinced that hedging was a zero-sum game. The CFO had his MBA and had been convinced by his professors that because prices followed a random walk, nobody could optimize around them. His approach was to hedge systematically and hope to achieve the average price over time. For reasons that we will explore later in the book, this CFO's methodology caused him to systematically underperform and resulted in hedging activities that were a consistent cost to his firm. But he does deserve credit for avoiding the mistake of hubris. He never tried to outthink the markets.

Other executives that Wayne observed believed they knew where prices would go; unfortunately, their views were almost always distorted with emotional bias. They weren't looking at price objectively and took excessive risks that often placed their firm on the verge of bankruptcy. Business failures caused by executives like these hurt more than investors. They also hurt their hard-working employees. Many employees get an important part of their compensation as equity in the company, and when that company goes bankrupt, their equity compensation becomes worthless. Working for a failing company is about more than simply losing one's job. Sad to say, we know many people who lost not only their jobs but their retirement nest eggs all at the same time—often when they thought they were nearing retirement.

Events like this motivated Wayne to find a way to improve management decisions. He began by taking a hard look at the ways one can estimate a market's expected distribution or range of prices and then set out to develop methodology and analytics that would empower executives with accurate and actionable information. Wayne thought option prices could provide the best estimate of what the market participants thought the price range would be. He had years of options experience, both as a trader and as the chairman of the settlement committee. During his time as a floor trader, Wayne did calculations every day to determine values and the settlement prices for options on NYMEX. Over time, he recognized that the option models, combined with user inputs to the model, implied an expected price range for the underlying commodity. It is that range that justified the price at which people bought and sold options. This price range estimate was unique in that it represented the consensus of the market. This estimate of price potential, one that is produced by the collective of all active market participants, is extremely valuable because it is objective, without individual bias, and is updated every trading day.

Initially, these estimates of price potential were used mainly to develop hedge strategies. Then one day Wayne took this concept to the next level, when he stopped thinking like a trader and began to think like an asset owner. He asked himself, If the options pricing models accurately estimate what could happen, couldn't we reverse engineer this so that asset owners could have an accurate understanding of how prices might affect their businesses in a way that was actionable, giving them time and the opportunity to protect themselves? How valuable would it be to businesses if options could be used to accurately estimate what might happen?

All of a sudden, Wayne had more than just a working range that was observed independently and objectively. By reverse engineering option prices, what traders believed about market potential was transformed into probability distributions of market prices. But now this information could be converted into probability distributions that estimated a firm's revenues and/or other financial metrics that it might use to make strategic decisions.

FAILURE BEGETS SUCCESS

Wayne realized that the clients of his original consultancy business asked him for help with the problems they knew they had but not with the ones they weren't aware of or thought unsolvable. It was only after something went wrong that Wayne's clients realized they had problems and reached out for help. He was certain that the typical approach to risk management used by most of these firms was inefficient and often ineffective. Wayne thought he could provide the firms with information that would help them to avoid the problems in the first place.

This led to the development of Wayne's patent, the Performance Risk Management system (US Patent 7,822,670 B2). Wayne's patented analytics are the foundation of PRM, which, through monthly reports that update a client's risk in budgetary terms, operates like a dynamic feedback loop that monitors new developments and updates the client on how changes might impact the performance of their business. The information contained in these monthly reports fills the ongoing needs of clients and has fueled the long-term success of Wayne's business.

NAVIGATING THROUGH THE DARKNESS

As the business grew, Andrew, who had been communicating with Wayne at arm's length, was brought into the fold of the consulting business, R^2. And since 2008, we have been working together full time, learning what customers need, building useful and innovative products, and enhancing our risk-management process along the way.

Put quite simply, our goal is to help businesses obtain and maintain clarity about their commodity price risk. Risked Revenue quantifies enterprise risk to ensure that each client's hedging activities and hedge portfolio is, and remains, aligned with its financial goals. When underlying business metrics are constantly changing and the business is vulnerable to setbacks or even failure because of price volatility, managers might feel as though they've been tasked with running around a completely darkened room in which they must avoid hitting the walls if they are to succeed.

Imagine yourself in that scenario of uncertainty. To protect yourself, you may decide to simply slow down. That would decrease the rate at which your underlying metric, your location, changes. And though this may succeed in making the run feel more like a walk, you are still moving around in a completely dark room, hoping that you don't run into a wall. You may have delayed and certainly lessened the impact, but you will still run into a wall because you haven't found a way to avoid them.

This book offers a better method for managing risk. Instead of your hedge program moving blindly in the darkness, we will give you and your business the tools needed to avoid the walls, and with them, disaster. Think of our tools as something that is literally as simple as a stick. You can pick a stick of arbitrary length and hold it out in front of you as you run around the room. Should that stick touch a wall, you'll have warning before you run into the wall. If you take appropriate action, you won't ever touch the wall. The stick is the tool and your awareness of whether the stick is touching the wall is the process.

BOOK OVERVIEW

At its core, *Risk Is an Asset* is a technical guide for specialists, CEOs, CFOs, and financial decision makers of all stripes—for any and all who fret over commodity price risk. This book will also serve MBA students well. It is filled with valuable lessons, groundbreaking analytics found nowhere else, and insights gleaned from decades of experience managing the risks associated with portfolios of physical assets, options, and futures. It is our collective experience that provided the foundation for, and inspired us to develop, our unique approach to commodities hedging.

This is a handbook that will help anyone responsible for managing, or who works for a firm exposed to, commodity price risk. If one thinks about it, gasoline has ethanol in it. Ethanol is made from corn. Biodiesel is made from soybeans, the source of soybean oil. The point is every commodity has a unique personality and is interrelated. And when commodity prices change, we describe that change as risk. It may vary somewhat from grains to metals to currencies to energy, but risk is risk. We measure it the same way and manage it the same way.

The tools developed to measure risk apply to any asset. This book provides you with a new way, one that we innovated, to look at risk and manage it at the enterprise level. It simply uses the old tools, which are useful in all commodities, in a new way.

While there is no guarantee that past performance will deliver future results, our risk advisory has helped several of our clients with various aspects of their risk management needs—trusted by S&P 500 companies, airlines, utilities, public and private E&P firms. Our contributions to their successes have been built on the simple idea that risk is an asset.

In the chapters that follow, we will demonstrate just how our philosophy and process plays out, with a particular focus on the distinction between strategic decisions, where we ask what you need or want, and tactical decisions, where we show you how to get it done. The first six chapters will introduce our approach and focus on the strategic considerations that will help you understand who should hedge. For those who should, we explain how to identify what, when, how much, and how to hedge. We'll clarify the difference between the old-school hedging and R^2's innovative approach, PRM, which focuses on meeting financial targets. And we'll show you how to quantify your risk in budgetary terms, implement a process to manage risk and measure your confidence for success.

Then, once we've got that groundwork covered, we'll expand the conversation to consider the following:

- how to organize your data

- how much data you need

- how to quantify your risk in actionable terms

Once a strategy has been selected, "Chapter Seven: Tactical Hedging" will show you the criteria we'd like you to consider when choosing which instruments to hedge with and how aggressive you might want to be when implementing the transactions. Then we will get down to business and discuss specific examples:

- how consumers hedge

- how producers hedge

- why hedging for manufacturers is different

- how hedging works in other industries

But before we start thinking about any of that, let's start by asking one simple question ... how is risk an asset?

Chapter Assets

- Process makes a complex and risky world manageable.

- Option prices provide a timely and objective measure of price potential.

- Price potential estimates can be used to stress test business performance.

- Process Risk Management manages risk to clearly defined targets.

- Process Risk Management ensures financial success.

CHAPTER ONE

Identifying and Managing Risk

*"Would you tell me, please, which way I
ought to go from here?" said Alice.*

"That depends a good deal on where you want to get to," said the cat.

—**Lewis Carroll**, *Alice in Wonderland*

RISK IS AN ASSET, but only when properly managed. To consider this more closely, if you were offered a chance to flip a coin, with heads meaning you get paid two times your bet and tails meaning you lose your bet, how much should you bet? If you don't flip the coin, you can't win *or* lose. Clearly, then, this opportunity is not an asset or a liability. If you bet everything you have on one coin toss, you could lose everything. Even though the expected value of that coin toss is positive, this betting strategy would be a liability, because there is a fifty-fifty chance you could lose everything. Neither of these strategies will turn this opportunity into an asset.

You could reduce the risk by half if you wagered just half of your wealth. This is a lot like a 50 percent hedge program—we know it helps but are not sure by how much. In this example, it is a lot easier to calculate. Imagine if you could bet half of your wealth once, and whether you won or lost, you could choose to do it again with the other half. Across these two bets the possible outcomes are as follows:

- head/head = 1 + 1 = win 2

- head/tail = 1 − 0.5 = win 0.5

- tail/head = −0.5 + 1 = win 0.5

- tail/tail = −0.5 − 0.5 = busted!

While this strategy improves your chances of success to 75 percent, you still have a 25 percent chance of flipping two tails in a row and getting wiped out. Maybe that's a risk you would be willing to accept, but we doubt many would risk everything even with those odds. Then again, if you are straight out of college with no family or other major responsibilities, maybe you flip the coin. On the other hand, if you are putting your kids through college and saving for retirement, we doubt that these odds would be acceptable.

But what if you could bet 10 percent of your wealth on each of ten individual bets? Now the only way you could lose all your money is to flip ten tails. The risk of wiping out is remotely small, 1/1,024 or 0.1 percent. More importantly, the probability of winning is attractively high, because all you need is four heads to be a net winner. The key here is that while the expected return of each coin flip remains the same, because you managed to keep the risk to acceptable levels, your probability of success has increased, and this opportunity is now an asset. If you split your wealth across twelve flips, the odds of busting fall to 1/4,096, and if you spread the risk across twenty flips, the odds fall to 1/1,048,576. Proactively choosing a risk threshold, one that fits your needs, allows you to turn risk into an asset. If you fail to quantify your choice and match it to your needs, you may guess right or you may not. Proactively choosing a risk threshold—one that fits your needs—allows you to turn risk into an asset.

Managing the risk to your tolerance is enough to turn this risk into an asset. But there is more: using a "smart stick" adds further improvement by adjusting the process to allow you to adjust your bets after each successive bet

> Proactively choosing a risk threshold—one that fits your needs—allows you to turn risk into an asset.

result. What if instead of betting 10 percent of your current worth across ten flips, you bet one-tenth of your risk on each of those ten bets? If your first bet was a winner, you'd bet more on the next bet. If it was a loser, you'd bet less. Using this process makes it impossible to go bankrupt, and, if you are lucky and throw six or more heads, adjusting your bets will leverage your success. Compare these two payout profiles below where both bettors start with $10 and flip a coin ten times:

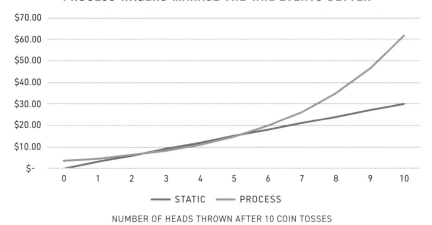

PROCESS WAGERS MANAGE THE TAIL EVENTS BETTER

NUMBER OF HEADS THROWN AFTER 10 COIN TOSSES

FIGURE 1-1

Using a process that adjusts your betting size after each coin result sacrifices some performance if you get only two, three, or four heads but outperforms when you do better or worse than that. In fact, the expected value of this strategy is improved.

Taking this back to a real-world scenario, you must take risks to grow. Imagine that you have a great business, but like most new businesses, it takes a while to get traction. Using PRM would make sure that your risk exposures are acceptable to you and will keep you in the game until conditions or performance improve. If you were fortunate enough to have things improve early, you could increase your risk acceptance immediately. If not, you would maintain an acceptable level of risk, one that would keep your doors open. *You* remain in control because your process allows you to manage your risk constantly and consistently. If you use PRM to maintain a Hedge Target, you will almost certainly achieve that target.

PRM PUTS YOU IN CONTROL

Imagine a world where you are always driving at the appropriate speed. Think about how safe you would be and the confidence you would enjoy when on the road. That kind of automation is coming with driverless cars. This technology is being implemented in Pittsburgh and other test cities. The media has reported some catastrophic accidents, but the number of these accidents will drop as technology improves. Eventually, driverless cars will have a better safety record than those driven by humans. For now, if you are the one involved in an accident with a driverless car, it is no consolation to be a statistic. But consider that every day you don't hear about a driverless car involved in a tragic accident, it means that safety standards are being raised and risk is being reduced. Automated driving is eventually going to replace humans and the number of accidents that humans experience along with it. When the "bugs" have been systematically removed, the number of accidents—and yes, fatal car accidents as well—will drop precipitously.

Software developers will learn from accidents to reinforce and improve safety. Experiences, a.k.a. real-time data, will be used to provide continuous feedback that enhances the system to prevent future accidents by improving the instructional code used by all cars. Specifically, the circumstances of every accident in the network will be reviewed. Adaptations will be made continuously to the whole network. Specific adjustments will also be made to adjust for unique neighborhood conditions, minimizing and perhaps eliminating the risk to the collective that makes up the driving universe.

PRM is the equivalent of your driverless car for hedging. Process Risk Management is an objective way to identify how to hedge at the appropriate time, in the appropriate amount, using the appropriate instruments based on the requirements of the hedger and the current conditions of the market. Supply and demand changes affect prices, which send signals to users and producers to slow down or ramp up consumption and production. These haven't, and won't, eliminate market price fluctuations. As long as there are price fluctuations, businesses will need to manage risk in response to those price movements. It is an agnostic process that objectively assesses the changes in price and tells you what is required for your business to achieve success. Process Risk Management provides you with a dashboard that alerts you to when defensive hedging is needed to keep your business safely on the road. It will allow you to avoid trips to the mechanic's shop … or a stay in the hospital.

PRM follows a process, but you make all the decisions. While the car may adjust for driving conditions, it doesn't adjust for your needs. Only *you* can do that. The driverless car's algorithm won't slow down when you want to enjoy the beautiful scenery on a backcountry road. Only you know what you want. By incorporating PRM into your hedge program, management will have a process that will alert them when adjustments should be considered. Some of these may be Risk Driven—defensive hedges that are needed to contain risk within your tolerance. Others may be Market Driven; that is, the price is too good to pass up because it brings measurable improvements to your projected performance. With PRM, *you* are in control!

THE DECISION PROCESS

Every decision that each person makes every day is unique. Given the same opportunity, different people won't make the same decision unless they have the same needs and want the same outcome. Think about what you had for breakfast today. If you chose to eat something nutritious, you are likely concerned about your overall health and therefore made your decision based on the risk of the consequences of unhealthy eating—obesity, heart disease, and diabetes just to name a few. Likewise, you probably dressed appropriately for the weather, knowing that being overdressed would lead to discomfort and distraction or being underdressed, in a worst-case scenario, could result in catching the flu.

Life is filled with hundreds of decisions every day. Each decision requires a new assessment of the circumstances so that adjustments can be made based on context and new inputs.

What you wear, what you eat, the direction you take to drive to a meeting—each one of these decisions comes down to employing a process to mitigate some specific risk. Life is filled with hundreds of decisions every day. Each decision requires a new assessment of the circumstances so that adjustments can be made based on context and new inputs.

Many decisions you make are stand-alone, one-time events. You eat this or that, exercise now or later. But others are linked together, with each decision based on the decisions you made earlier. The collective of these can be thought of as a decision *process*. Consider this: After you start your car's engine, the first thing you do is listen to determine if the engine is running properly. Then you glance at the car's dashboard. Red dashboard lights identify the things you should fix or check before getting on the road. No red lights means the risk of car trouble is unlikely, and you are good to go. But the process does not stop there. Once on the road, you employ process to observe and adapt your driving behavior in a way that allows you to respond to risks as they present themselves. Whenever you come to a red traffic light or stop sign, you stop and wait until it is safe to proceed through the intersection.

A simple question might be, "How fast is a safe speed for me to drive?" At first glance, everyone would probably agree that driving at 30 mph is a safe speed. But is it always? What if you were driving at 30 mph on the interstate when traffic was flowing at the speed limit, probably more than double your speed? Cruising along much slower than the drivers around you would only create a hazard to yourself and everyone else. Let's also consider when you are driving down a road you travel often and know well. Do you drive the same speed on a dark, rainy night as you do on a bright, sunny day? We hope not, for your sake and the sake of other drivers.

When you put distance between you and the car in front of you, when you place both hands on the steering wheel while being passed by a massive semitruck, when you flip down your sun visor so you can see the road better, you are essentially hedging against a potential risk. What you would never do is routinely set the cruise control to the posted speed limit, regardless of the traffic or weather conditions. That would put you at greater risk because useful information was ignored, which would compromise your ability to steer and stop.

RANDOMNESS IS NOT WITHOUT CHARACTER

Most people say that the markets are a random walk; like the weather, they are unpredictable and uncertain. And so most people just assume that they should behave the same way toward the markets every day. That doesn't exactly make sense to us. The markets *are* a random walk, just like the weather. However, you shouldn't respond to the markets in the same way each day, just like you shouldn't waste the time and energy to bring an umbrella with you everywhere you go, no matter the weather conditions. The weather may be unpredictable, but only to an extent. Seasonal patterns dominate. Summer temperature ranges are higher than winter ranges. Who doesn't wear lighter clothing in the summer than in the winter? Within each season, good forecast data and short-term trends can help you estimate the likelihood of getting rained on to a high degree of certainty. And in the cases of major shifts in weather patterns or sudden disasters such as tornadoes, hurricanes, or blizzards, your umbrella won't be enough to keep you safe, warm, and dry. Significant weather events happen. Fortunately, we do not have to face them very often.

Evaluating the climate of the market and your company's exposure to risk is just like evaluating the weather. Someone living in Houston has little need for an overly insulated home or a set of snowshoes for a blizzard. But Houstonians do need to worry about scorching heat and hurricanes or, at the very least, heavy rains that can cause flooding. No matter where in the world we live, we are aware that we need to prepare and protect ourselves from the weather, based on our unique location and circumstances.

So asking the question, "Who should manage risk?" is like asking, "Who should prepare for inclement weather?" The answer is everyone—each for their own circumstances and each in their own way. Everyone needs to manage risk, but not everyone needs to hedge. At least not in the common meaning of the word. Just as car insurance doesn't protect drivers from every possible risk, neither does hedging. Sometimes other tools are more appropriate, but we don't know which tool is most appropriate until we understand how risk might affect us.

NOT WHO, BUT WHAT, WHEN, HOW MUCH, AND HOW?

In its simplest form, to find the correct answer to the question of who should hedge really boils down to identifying one's risk and risk tolerance. How much risk exposure is too much, for an individual and for a company? Everybody needs to assess risk. You need to make sure that you don't have more risk than you can handle. If you can handle the risk, then you don't need to hedge. If you do have more risk than you can tolerate, what does that mean? That means that a single negative event could have a crippling effect on your business—from exceeding your credit limits, to forced layoffs, to failing to meet budget terms, even to bankruptcy.

There are a lot of companies that are overexposed. They haven't shielded themselves from risk because they've underestimated it and haven't hedged. But there are also companies that think they have more risk than they do. Often these firms are overhedged. Just because you are exposed to commodity price fluctuations doesn't necessarily mean that you should or need to hedge. As we will see in the following examples, sometimes hedging is not the appropriate way to manage risk.

A Matter of Accounting

In the oil collapse from 2008 into 2009, we had two national retail gasoline chains call us for hedging help. Year in and year out, they held plenty of gasoline in inventory. Think about it: there's always gasoline for sale at the pumps; they never go dry. So to sell gasoline, there's always going to be some minimum threshold held in inventory.

Looking at that stored gas, they were reasoning like this: We bought our inventory five years ago, when this gas was worth one dollar per gallon. When the value rose to three dollars per gallon, we thought we profited by two dollars per gallon. Then from 2008 to 2009, the price plummeted back down to one dollar per gallon, so we now lost two dollars per gallon.

Instead, we proposed looking at their business another way, one where their commodity price risk was managed through their normal operations. Because this firm had been accounting for the held inventory using the "last in, first out" (LIFO) method, they found themselves reporting large gains on their original inventory as prices went up and large losses as prices fell down. If instead they had used the "first in, first out" (FIFO) method, this procedural switch would embed weekly price changes in their weekly sales. Given the high turnover rate of inventory, this would spread a series of small price changes over the sale of multiple millions of gallons of gasoline. A simple change in accounting methods would have mitigated the perceived loss, and the financials of these firms would more accurately represent their performance.

These gasoline retailers didn't need to hedge in the traditional manner. Instead they needed to focus on managing inventory turnover as the best method for containing price risk. To support this effort, the simplest and most effective thing they could do was change their accounting methodology. Of course, if they didn't change the accounting method, then hedging would have helped. But this would, in fact, add risk to their operations, because it would expose them to fixed prices for longer periods of time. Each day, these firms balance the volume of gas they buy with the gas they sell to the customers who drive up to fill their cars. When these volumes are balanced and the selling price is adjusted at the pump each day, these firms do not have meaningful price risk.

If they chose to stay with LIFO accounting, hedging would have managed the risk, but that would have been a lot of effort for no measurable gain.

Organizational Structure Matters

In the US, we have several breakfast cereal giants that are focused on sourcing the grains for their cereals at a level that allows them to keep their pricing competitive. They can pass these costs, and changes in costs, through to the consumer. In other industries, like petrochemical companies making polypropylene for plastic bottles and other items, this is what they almost always do. But cereal manufacturing is a mature business with small profit margins. To remain competitive, they find themselves in a constant search looking for any strategic advantage.

Typically, these organizations are extremely large—so large, in fact, that it is nearly impossible for them to coordinate the efforts of each segment of their business in real time. To be responsive to changing market conditions, firms of this size will often be organized into multiple business units that support and depend upon each other. At the beginning of each business year, the part of the organization responsible for buying the grain will establish budgetary goals for themselves. Their primary focus might be to maintain a steady flow of grain feedstocks and, secondarily, to buy them at or below a specific price. Managers are their boots on the ground and in the best position to ensure their unit will achieve the unit's budgetary targets. This budget or goal was coordinated with the budgets of other departments, like the one responsible for the fuel and all related manufacturing costs, so that collectively their efforts would result in another profitable year. Essentially, when an organization gets large enough, it must often segment responsibility for managing each of these different business units that collectively are their business.

This business structure allows each division to manage its own business. Now, a hedge program would allow each of these organizations to optimize around the specific budgetary objectives dictated by the corporation. And so, while a smaller company with a less complicated organization, like a petrochemical business, can use estimates of enterprise performance to manage risk from the top down, large conglomerates, like breakfast cereal manufacturers, often can't do that because they are too complex to coordinate business unit activities in real time. Instead, they look at the success of each business unit. The key to their success is that the specific metrics set up for those business units are coordinated with the other business units to achieve success for the parent holding company. If everyone does their jobs, the organization is successful. When a unit is troubled, timely reports make it possible to adjust.

In this scenario, hedging at the business unit level might make complete sense. If every unit achieves budget, the parent company will have a successful year. On the other hand, if the feedstocks are handed off from business unit to business unit—and the cost with it—so that the variable price of the grain is included in, or insignificant to, the retail price of every box of cereal, then hedging is not warranted.

A Burning Desire to Hedge

The CFO of a company that owns 150 supermarkets with fresh bakeries in each one called Wayne one day and said, "My boss wants a hedge program for the natural gas that we're burning to run these bakeries."

Clearly, they were burning a lot of natural gas to keep all those ovens going. During their discussion, Wayne asked him how much gas they burn and how much money the company made in a year. As it turned out, the money they were spending for gas was so small, it was a rounding error when compared to the firm's profitability.

Wayne said, "Well, here's the problem. You're only burning about a million dollars a year worth of gas. And if you're going to run a hedge program around that gas, you're going to chew up a lot of your time. You're going to have to expand your credit capacity and dedicate time to doing business with other companies. And you're going to have to pay us to help you do it. You're probably going to spend $200,000 a year managing a commodity that you're spending $1 million a year on. More importantly, you probably only have, in most years, $300,000 of risk around that million dollars of fuel cost. That's a thirty percent volatility estimate. To me, all you're going to do is make an awful lot of work for yourself for very little benefit. And by the way, let me ask you: why do you burn that much fuel?"

"It's because we leave the ovens on 24-7," replied the CFO.

"Are your stores open 24-7?" asked Wayne.

"Well, no, they're not."

"Then why don't you shut them down at some point in the afternoon and just cut your fuel costs down by thirty percent because you're only burning them sixteen hours a day instead of twenty-four hours a day?"

"I guess we could do that. Great idea!" exclaimed the CFO.

The bottom line for this firm is that the amount of fuel they were burning relative to the size of the organization was de minimis. The amount of money it costs to run a hedge program relative to the amount of risk they had around how much fuel they're burning was excessive and disproportionate. There was no way that managing price risk with a hedge program was going to have a beneficial impact. The question that should be answered is whether changing operational procedures made economic sense.

WHEN PRICE IS REALLY, REALLY IMPORTANT

Now that we have provided examples of firms that should manage risk but should not hedge, let's talk about firms that *should* hedge. For example, consider this: In 2014, West Texas Intermediate (WTI), a grade of crude oil used to benchmark oil prices, was above one hundred dollars. Producers, all of them, were profitable and enjoying prosperity. Yet this was a time when many producers were hesitant to hedge. Instead of locking in great returns, many reduced the size of their hedge portfolios. Why? Some might have thought that oil prices, in their fourth consecutive year above $90/bbl., were stable and hedging was unnecessary. Others were probably uncomfortable with the forward price of oil swaps. Used by producers to hedge, swap prices for the following years, 2015 and 2016, were deeply discounted at the time. Hedging forward was only possible if a producer was willing to accept a discount of 5–10 percent on the price of oil.

> If your commodity price exposure can threaten your profit margin, you will almost certainly need a hedge program.

What's the litmus test you should use to determine whether your company needs to hedge? If your commodity price exposure can threaten your profit margin, you will almost certainly need a hedge program.

In hindsight, producers never should have reduced their hedging activities, and those price discounts they balked at were minor when compared to the ensuing price decline. Over the course of the next year, oil prices fell so persistently that at the bottom there were a total of eighteen days during which WTI traded below $30.00/bbl. Oil prices averaged $33.45/bbl. during the first quarter of 2016, about 30 percent lower than in the year before and 66 percent below the price two years earlier. These low prices slashed producer revenues, forcing many firms to burn through cash reserves to maintain operations.

A few producers, on the other hand, were not only profitable, they put themselves in an advantageous position as prices fell. They maintained adequate hedges as prices collapsed by remaining focused on price potential and continuously managing their risk. As prices fell, they could see that the likelihood of achieving budgetary targets was eroding. In response, they prudently added new hedges. Hedging as prices fell may have been difficult, but it was necessary. The new hedges enabled them to stabilize revenues and achieve budgetary success.

So how did these producers know that adding hedges at lower prices was a good idea? How did they determine how much additional protection they needed and at what cost? More importantly, what process did this group of producers use to identify that they needed more hedges and had the confidence to do so?

Now that we have discussed identifying risk, let's move on to discuss something even more difficult for many companies … facing the facts.

Chapter Assets

- Everyone needs to manage risk; only some firms need to hedge.

- If commodity risk exceeds profit margins, you probably need a hedge process.

- Metrics expressed in budgetary terms are needed to determine if risk levels are acceptable.

- PRM will help you respond to changing market conditions— either the hedges you need (Risk Driven) or want (Market Driven).

CHAPTER TWO

Facing the Facts

You absolutely cannot make a series of good decisions
without first confronting the brutal facts.

—James C. Collins

WHILE SERVING AS THE RISK MANAGER for a half dozen options traders on the trading floor, Andrew noticed that the portfolio for one of his traders contained a large position in one particular month at one particular strike price. This was concerning because one of the first signs of potential trouble is a larger-than-normal option position in a commodity that is not moving. When asked, the trader casually mentioned it was not a problem because all the veteran traders in the pit had the same position. That was the moment when the hair on Andrew's neck stood up. He knew instantly that this was no longer just a problem. *It was a big problem!* Andrew explained that because all the traders shared the same position, there was a much greater liability than the traders were aware of, regardless of their experience. Everyone was stuck. And it was only going to get worse. The way to manage the position was to halt any increases and trim it down as soon as possible. The conclusion was that the position became an albatross for all the traders in the pit. Andy's advice to reduce the position quickly, regardless of the losses, was necessary to avoid much bigger losses.

Fast-forward to April 2008, when Andrew was interviewing with Wayne to join his company. Wayne had Andrew read *Good to Great* by Jim Collins. One of the big epiphanies of the book was that successful companies managed their business by "confronting the brutal facts." It was an articulation of risk management that both of us had been practicing as traders since the beginning. Collins found that the companies that survived and thrived were the ones who took their risk head-on. For example, Eastman Kodak had to confront the brutal fact that digital photography was replacing film. The faster it reacted (Kodak invented the first digital camera!), the smaller the losses, and if it was clever enough, the firm could turn lemons into lemonade by trailblazing digital anew. But management balked, and the company that was in the Dow Jones Industrial Average for seventy-four years paid the ultimate price by going bankrupt. Perhaps they should have remembered the words of Robert Frost, who wrote, "The best way out is always through."

In terms of managing risk for a business whose costs or revenue is highly exposed to fluctuating prices, if you are not confronting the brutal facts about higher cost potential or lower revenue potential, price risk will rear its ugly head at the worst possible

> If you are not confronting the brutal facts about higher cost potential or lower revenue potential, price risk will rear its ugly head at the worst possible time with the worst possible consequences.

time with the worst possible consequences. Conversely, the active management of risk on a continuing basis will nip problems in the bud.

We had a joke on the exchange floor: Want to have a large trading error? Start out with a small one. This was why the rule of trading errors was to cover (liquidate) the error immediately. While the evidence is hearsay, every error we observed went from bad to worse when the owner did not address it immediately. The lessons in risk management are just as straightforward. Either manage risk proactively or someone else may end up managing it for you reactively.

By actively managing risk, you keep risk decisions small and the subsequent decisions even smaller. For the car driver, keep your hands on the steering wheel and always keep your eyes on the road. For the business with commodity exposure, keep updating your risk and always confront the brutal facts.

TRADING DIRTY SOCKS

Back when Wayne was making the commute for that three-hour class on trading in New York City, the instructor said something interesting during his lecture one day that Wayne never forgot: "I could trade dirty socks if there was a market in dirty socks."

Wayne's instructor was referring to the features of commodities that, once understood, make them universal in terms of trading. Whether we're talking about stocks, bonds, currencies, crude oil, natural gas, cotton, coffee, sugar, gold, silver, heating oil, or gasoline, the important concept here is that everything that gets traded has a unique risk profile and an individual rhythm that a trader needs to understand. For example, natural gas typically has its greatest spikes in activity in the months November through January, from the onset of winter through most of the winter months. Then, by the time that winter is winding down, there's more certainty about how the rest of the season will play out. To invoke a gambling metaphor, there aren't as many cards left to turn over.

There are nuances that are unique to each commodity. Cotton is an agricultural commodity, so there will always be issues that arise dependent upon the season and the weather. Similarly, for coffee, everyone watches the crop progress in Brazil. And when it comes to oil and gasoline, an OPEC meeting can certainly influence the price of these commodities. In other words, there are individual influences that shape the character of each commodity. And so, when Wayne's instructor talked about trading dirty socks, what he was implying was this: once the individual nature of a commodity, no matter how unlikely, was understood, it would suddenly become just like any other tradable commodity.

This concept would eventually help us lay the foundation for R^2's hedging model. With our backgrounds in engineering and science, we understood that a useful model would update objectively and periodically by managing dynamic inputs. When engineers deal with dynamic inputs—data that's always changing—one of the biggest challenges is determining how the model is going to respond to fluctuations.

The same goes for hedgers. To achieve success, you need to be smart about how often you're reacting to the market. Our insight was that the commodities market prices have data dynamics not unlike those dealt with in many engineering problems. Risk, after all, is always changing.

And that meant that we could apply the same management philosophy and risk analytics to different markets and businesses.

With the foundation to our new model in place, we went on to establish four key principles upon which we built our success, principles that we believe set our approach apart from the other risk-management firms.

Principle 1: Think Independently

One of the keys to the continued success of our company is that we value and support independent thinking throughout our firm. In the classroom, we were never the kind of students who were taught something and then held it in such reverence that we would never deviate. The independent streak we have in common may have played a large part in attracting each of us to floor trading. Once there, our learning curve was like drinking from a fire hose. Things happen very quickly on the floor. Floor traders make hundreds of decisions every day. You must think quickly and act decisively, or you'll miss opportunities. It became apparent that survival required that we think independently.

On the floor, you had to make sure that you weren't going to get trampled by the herd. Many times, when other traders were going left, the best thing you could do was go right. There were definite advantages to being alone in a trade. Because when trades get crowded and everyone has the same position, you will have a lot of competition when you want to get out. Parachutes are very expensive when demand exceeds supply.

We created PRM to help clients maintain objectivity and perspective, the underpinnings of independent thought. Thinking independently requires the collection of objective data and the ability to organize it in ways specifically related to your measures of success. Only then can you truly confront the brutal facts. Thinking independently means having the strength and confidence to seek out what is correct for you, whether or not that is accepted by others.

Principle 2: Maintain Perspective

This principle is universal in risk management. All perspective means is that, in any given moment, you make sure to stay focused on and take care of the biggest issue first. For example, if you are a producer with 80 percent of revenues from oil and 20 percent from natural gas, you've got to be managing the oil risk first. Then, when you're done managing the oil risk, if you still have too much risk, you can look at the gas risk.

The same principle applied when we were on the trading floor. What were the most significant holdings in the portfolios we were managing? How might they be affected by the market? How much risk did we have, and which strategies were moving the needle the most? Which positions in our options portfolios were likely to give us the biggest headache ... or potentially the greatest reward? It was important that smaller issues in our portfolios were relegated to the back burner.

On the floor, there are many, many variables that could push you around: news items that change the direction of the market or the way order flow might affect volatility. There were certain days where the direction of the market mattered more than volatility. And then there were those days where the volatility mattered more than the direction of the market. A good trader is constantly prioritizing, making sure that he maintains a perspective that allows him to focus on what matters most on any given day.

And by the very nature of perspective, people in different positions can see the same fluctuation in the market very differently. The price of oil going from $40/bbl. to $60/bbl. is great for the buyer but not the seller. Similarly, financial traders have a short-term focus, and our clients, the asset owners, have another much longer time horizon. At least, they *should* have a different focus than the traders. The problem for asset managers is that most of the information they receive is appropriate for traders. It is probably good information, but the information is never put in the context of the asset managers' business performance.

We've observed CEOs who would not put on a hedge because they were holding out for an extra quarter or fifty cents per barrel, seemingly unaware that their firm was incredibly at risk and that an extra fifty cents per barrel was meaningless. For example, imagine the market recently rallied from $40/bbl. to $60/bbl., the best price anyone has seen in a year, yet the CEO wants $61/bbl. In that instance, we would try to get him to change his perspective and stop looking at the numbers like a trader. "No, no. You're $20/bbl. better off than you were two months ago. By holding out for sixty-one dollars, you may be risking many dollars to gain one dollar. Sixty dollars is a great price. The speculators are all long, and the downside is now greater than the upside. You need to take some risk off the table right away."

The whole purpose of the analytics we provide is to help clients focus on information that is *meaningful* to their business. It doesn't mean that other things, like a news headline or what the three-day moving average is doing, aren't important. They simply are not of primary importance to the client. Focusing on secondary or lessor issues is a distraction. Management needs to know and monitor what is important to them.

> The whole purpose of the analytics we provide is to help clients focus on information that is meaningful to their business.

To provide an illustration, what our clients basically need to know might look like this: Given the current state of global economics, it's unlikely that the annual average of natural gas prices are going over $3.50/MMBtu in the near future. Likewise, it is unlikely that they would go below $2.00/MMBtu. So with an estimated working range between $2.00/MMBtu and $3.50/MMBtu, the midpoint is $2.75/

MMBtu. While the midpoint is unlikely to be the average, it is a reasonable estimate of what the average might be. So any time gas goes above $2.75/MMBtu, as an asset owner, they should be thinking about locking in the price on some of this natural gas. And any time it dips below $2.75/MMBtu, they should realize that they might be selling it too cheap. Below $2.75, if they can tolerate the risk, it probably makes sense for them to look for ways to be patient. It's all about perspective. And that perspective constantly needs to be updated because it will likely change.

There's a fitting story related to psychologist Danny Kahneman, who partnered with Amos Tversky, a brilliant mathematician. The two worked closely together throughout their lives, dedicated to understanding human cognitive bias and handling of risk. Danny and Amos were in graduate school here in the States when they suddenly had to return home to Israel to fight in the Six-Day Arab-Israeli War in June of 1967.

This story is about the first assignment given to Danny. The military needed more officers and needed to improve the way they selected young cadets in training school to become officers. Prior to this assignment, the Israeli Air Force had been selecting candidates by subjecting them to a difficult team test and observing qualities like who took charge, was submissive, was stubborn, was arrogant, was patient, or was a quitter. Under the stress of the event, it was felt that each man's true nature was revealed. The impression of each candidate's character was direct and compelling. The military had no trouble choosing which men would make good officers and which would not. The problem surfaced when outcomes were compared to predictions—how the candidates actually performed in officer training. The predictions were worthless.

The hard part, Danny reasoned out, was how to get an accurate measure of a candidate's character. He was aware of the halo effect, which had been described back in 1915 by an American psychologist named Edward Thorndike. Thorndike asked US Army officers to rate their men according to some physical trait and then assess on a series of less tangible qualities. What he found was that interviewers were influenced by a feeling created when assessing the candidate's first quality, and that feeling would bleed over into the second and other qualities.

Danny decided he must find a way to minimize the halo effect during interviews. He told the interviewers to put a list of questions to each recruit designed to determine not how a person thought about themselves but how the person behaved—not what the interviewer thought of the candidate but what the candidate actually accomplished. The interviewers hated these changes because they thought they were being turned into robots and were being robbed of their ability to exercise their expertise.

The new test scores were a success. They predicted the likelihood that a recruit would be successful at any job. It gave the Israeli army a better idea than it had before of who would succeed as an officer. In fact, the *process* that Danny created proved to be so successful that the Israeli military, with minor modifications, still employs it today.

> If you use the wrong data or metric, you may not get bad results, but you're not going to improve your chances of getting the results you want.

What Kahneman and Tversky demonstrated through their lifetime of research reinforces our second principle: maintain perspective. If you use the wrong data or metric, you may not get bad results, but you're not going to improve your chances of getting the results you want.

Principle 3: Use Your Risk Map

To quote the great philosopher Yogi Berra, "If you don't know where you are going, you'll end up someplace else."

Oftentimes, the senior staff for a firm that produces a commodity will look at the current price, assume that is the price they will get, and plot their course forward under the assumption they will achieve their financial goals. They never ask themselves how much prices might fall or rise and consider the consequences. To create your risk map, first employ an objective procedure for risking the price(s), *then* ask yourself what would happen to your company's performance should that happen. Most companies don't bother to think about what their business will look like if they have to survive a period of challenging prices. What would our producer's revenues or free cash flow look like if prices fell 25 percent? Would their cash flow be compromised? Would they be able to meet their debt covenants?

Leaving the world of commodities aside for a moment, I'm sure you, like most people, have some savings. How do you risk your savings? Do you measure that risk in dollars or time? We agree that you must keep track of your savings in dollars but ask whether this is the only metric useful to you. Did you ever take the time to think about what would happen if you lost your job and didn't have any income? That's the real risk you are preparing for with savings. If you lost your job, you might be fine for a month or two, but what if it took twelve months to find a new job? Considering the adjustments you can and can't make to your spending habits, how long would your savings last? Expressing your savings in months of spending is an important metric. Shouldn't you know if you can expect your savings to last six months but that you would be in trouble by month seven? Losing your job is an issue. Not finding a new job for twelve months is an enormous issue. If you know how long your savings will last, you will have a relative idea of how large your resources are and whether your savings meet your needs.

That's why it is essential to create what we call a risk map. It is the foundation for Principle 2, which posits we always need to keep perspective of our biggest issue first. But how could you possibly know how to handle the biggest issue if you don't really know how big a risk it and other issues are?

When creating a risk map, you should consider the following: Where do you want to go? How are you going to get there? What are the perils that you might face? Where exactly is your company on this risk map? Could it be closer to the edge of a cliff than you think? Be sure to build your risk map using meaningful analytics and explore the range of unanticipated but possible events that you may encounter. Give careful consideration to which risks are important and how you need to measure those risks. Then identify where your stress points are and the resources you have at your disposal. Working with your risk map over time, you'll see that it is a feedback loop that adjusts for changing business conditions, both internal and external. You will develop the confidence to make strategic adjustments and changes when they are appropriate. You will respond proactively. Your risk map is your guide to optimal performance and financial success.

Principle 4: Develop a Culture That Seeks Success

Everything in our business starts with culture. Culture is the personality of your company. The company's mission, values, ethics, expectations, and goals are established by management but communicated through culture. It defines the environment in which employees work. A positive culture with a solid ethos is the lowest common denominator in terms of performance. If you take care of and respect your employees, your employees will respect and take care of your customers.

The ethos of any company starts at the top. Wayne's first business model proved to be less than perfect, and he lost several clients because he solved their problems. He did not want to become an out-and-out salesman. That might lead to his needing to ask clients to buy products and services whether they really needed them or not. Instead, he decided to create a product and build an organization that provided information that customers needed to know. And based on that model, one inspired by Wayne's ethos, Risked Revenue gets paid not for the hours worked or how often clients use the information they're provided with, but for simply delivering the information they need to use as they see fit. This value-driven approach to client relationships is one way Wayne's firm differentiates itself from other advisers.

We are incentivized to help companies build and maintain successful hedge programs. If they don't need to hedge, we don't ask them to hedge. And we don't want them to hedge any more than they must or any more than they should. Our culture focuses on identifying meaningful metrics for each client and delivering accurate information so that they are in a position to make the best decisions. If the best decision is not to hedge, that's fine with us. That is precisely why we think of ourselves as risk advisers and *not* hedge advisers.

Give the customers what they ask for, then tell them what they need to know.

We get paid for delivering valuable analytics and good advice so our clients can make decisions that will serve their company needs. This is so

42

embedded in our ethos, we have a quote for it: "Give the customers what they ask for, then tell them what they need to know." What does that mean? When we find our customers looking at their risk from a perspective that doesn't exactly match their needs, we first answer their questions. And then if, because of our experience, we recognize that there is another, more insightful way to consider this problem or opportunity, we make sure that they have that information too. Our responsibility is to provide all the information they need before they make any decision. And at the end of the day, it's always the client's decision to make.

Ours is a culture that seeks to establish a collaborative relationship with each client in our efforts to help them succeed. Their solvency, if not success, means we can continue to advise them on risk. We try to establish relationships that make us nonequity partners with our clients, putting us on the same side of the negotiation table with them. When we reach out to a client, they know we're only calling because there's something they need to hear. This makes the process very efficient for both of us and builds trust. Our annual retention rate of 98 percent since inception speaks volumes not only to the level of their confidence in our work, but to the results PRM and our analytics helped them to achieve over time.

Risk is a powerful tool for driving business success—if you create a culture within your organization that is focused on and willing to manage the risk. Culture that seeks success, combined with an accurate risk map, will allow your firm to build consensus and elevate its confidence that the proactive management of risk will ensure financial success.

And with all that established, the question becomes, What exactly does success look like?

Chapter Assets

- How do we measure success? Think independently; remain objective.

- Maintain perspective and manage the largest risks first.

- Create your risk map.

- Develop a culture to focus on your success metrics.

CHAPTER THREE

Hedging Risk to Achieve Success

Two roads diverged in a wood, and I—I took the one less traveled by, and that has made all the difference.

—Robert Frost

WHAT MIGHT HEDGING ACCOMPLISH?

Imagine you are the CEO of W&A Resources. You'd like to convince management that hedging will go a long way to making the company stable and stronger. With hedges, the company could avoid cash flow squeezes that might lead to budget cuts and layoffs. The firm has worked hard over the years to acquire some of the best talent in the industry. You consider these people to be a key asset. Losing them would be like trying to win an auto race with a flat tire. You might still win the race if you can limp over the finish line, but only if you are close to it. If that flat occurs early in the race, you either fix it or you've lost. In your company, there remains a lot of work to do; you are not close to the finish line. You need the firm to be running smoothly. For that to happen, you must keep the firm financially strong and avoid the risk of cutbacks that might force you to release talented people. Then you will have every expectation that the firm will be successful.

How do you build consensus within your firm and at the board of directors level? It might be that several of your board members don't want to hedge. They have stated that they, and many of the firm's investors, are in this because they believe energy prices will go higher. They want to own the risk so that when prices rally, there will be a *big* payday. You appreciate their view but instinctively know the firm has too much risk. If prices tumble, it will be very difficult to meet all the firm's financial obligations. If prices stay low for a long time, there is no telling how bad things could get. If you could identify precisely how much your firm needs to hedge and the benefit those hedges would deliver, then you might convince management that the upside on the remaining production that was not hedged would still be enough for that *big* payday when prices rally.

You might instinctively know that you need to hedge but just aren't sure how much. How much risk is too much? How much is just right? And if you do need to hedge, how do you communicate the need for and value of the hedges to other decision makers at this firm? Finally, once hedged, what metric(s) should be used to determine the effectiveness of the hedge?

There is a way.

HEDGING AS A PROCESS

Similar to the way we manage our lives, a firm's exposure to commodity price risk should be managed with PRM. Process is a feedback loop that takes in all relevant information and identifies how much risk your firm has and the cost/benefit of hedging. When risk is measured in budgetary terms, the analytics will allow you to match your risk tolerance to the condition of the market. You'll be able to coordinate your hedge activities with your budgetary goals. And most importantly, by using a *process*, you can monitor the impact that market changes have on your expected performance and identify changes in your hedge strategy needed to ensure success. PRM will indicate whether and when more hedges are needed. You'll be able to assure stakeholders that in bad times you will have the hedges you need and in good times that it is unlikely that you will be overhedged. There are three elements that must be quantified to ensure that PRM creates an opportunity to build an appropriate and effective hedge program.

Portfolio Dynamics

Portfolio dynamics measures the risk to your asset(s) and the cost of your supply or value of production, both today and for the foreseeable future. Basically, it estimates how good or bad things might get. Think of these expressed in budgetary terms, not simply in cost per unit like dollars per barrel. This analysis begins with risking price, then calculating the total cost or revenues, and can then be further modified to show the impact on financial metrics like free cash flow, EBITDA, or debt/EBITDA ratios. You will need to know both the current tradable price(s) and estimates for possible or risked prices. This will allow you to stress test your business. We will discuss risking prices later in the book. For now, imagine looking at your business performance in three cases—High, Base, and Low Case—to estimate the range of performance outcomes you can expect … and should prepare for.

Risk Tolerance Metrics

Risk tolerance identifies the limits for budgetary metrics that you are willing to endure: How much change in the value of your assets is desirable and acceptable? Essentially, this defines the risk appetite of your organization. Is the Low Case too low or the High Case too high? To answer that question, you express risk using the same metrics that drive your success. Would your business survive if prices were unattractive? For how long? Risk tolerance is specific to each organization and will vary over time as market conditions, your organization's resources, and the amount of leverage it uses changes.

Market Opportunities

Market opportunities are how current prices might allow you to exploit or protect the cost of goods or value of an asset. Based on the pricing available, what is the smartest thing you can do today, either defensively or opportunistically?

The next step is to pull all three elements together and generate an accurate risk assessment for your firm—your risk map. By looking at your portfolio dynamics, we're going to begin by quantifying your risk in budgetary terms. Then we're going to figure out what your risk tolerance is based on how you measure success and your comfort level. Your comfort level will be directly impacted by market opportunities, which will dictate whether you should act now or remain confident that you can continue to monitor your risk over time.

To illustrate how two similar entities might have very different risk tolerances, take, for example, two people recently out of college, both making $70,000 a year. The risk profile might be the same for both. They could get a 10 percent raise next year or they could lose their job. However, the risk *tolerance* is probably different for each of them. Especially if one person has saved $20,000 in the bank and the other one hasn't.

The person with $20,000 saved is more than likely going to have a higher risk tolerance for losing their job than the one who doesn't have any money saved. But if the person with money saved has a family and kids, they might have less risk tolerance for losing the job because of these dependents.

These factors are the ones they are dealing with today, but we must also consider anticipated changes. Perhaps one of them has a contract to buy a home or is expecting a child. Either event, once it transpires, will have a meaningful impact on risk tolerance

The portfolio dynamics are the part of risk that we must quantify to understand where the risk is coming from and how much is at risk. Risk tolerance isn't just a number; it's determined by all the resources available to the firm to handle adversity. Risk tolerance is directly impacted by the tools that a company has available to handle the worst-case scenario—things like adjustments to spending, available credit, access to capital infusions, and the capacity to hedge.

If these elements are inadequate to manage the potential risk, then we should consider strategic changes and hope for better market opportunities that would allow us to prepare for an adverse outcome. Ultimately, risk must be reduced to within tolerance to ensure success.

RISK IS AN ASSET

Just like everybody has risk, everybody must work. We work so we can earn a living. Our salary provides a home, food, and quality of life for ourselves and our families. Assuming we have a secure position, our only risk associated with work is commuting to work from home and then back each day. If we wanted to have zero traveling risk, we'd live at the office. But we don't live at the office because we want to have quality of life. We want to spend time with our family and friends.

When it comes to the risk of getting to work, we hope you'll agree that risk is an asset. It enables us to meet our needs and our families' needs. But this risk isn't the same for each of us, and risk itself can change with time. So how do you determine how much risk you have and what you should do to manage it?

Let's look at the following example: If you live in the northern US, based upon which season it is (your immediate financial situation), you may need to take extra precautions (hedge) to protect your asset—that of ensuring you arrive to work on time every day. During the summer, for example, the weather is generally sunny and predictable (a robust financial picture), so making it to work on time is of minimal concern and takes little preparation (minimal hedging strategies). However, when winter arrives, suddenly the same drive becomes less predictable and more unstable. You may be concerned that on any given day you could face blizzard-like conditions, which would cause you to miss work. In this case, it would be wise to invest in more measures, like snow tires, warm clothing, emergency equipment, and leaving yourself lots of extra travel time, because you cannot afford to miss work.

Now imagine that the standard practice is to simply have all-weather tires on your vehicle and leave yourself an extra half hour to get to work every day. Does this strategy make much sense? It will work some of the time, but in the spring, summer, and fall months, you are needlessly arriving to work much earlier than necessary, losing valuable time that you could be spending with your family. You are effectively overhedging. Conversely, during the winter, snow tires and thirty extra minutes might not be enough to ensure you make it to work on time.

This kind of broad-stroke approach to preparing for weather is very much like the old-school approach to hedging. The tactic was simply to *reduce* risk—usually by a fixed percentage. You might say that you're going to hedge in order to neutralize half of your existing risk. Or a quarter. In either case it's arbitrary because you never asked, "How much risk do I have in the first place?" Without knowing that, you can't know how much risk you will be left with after hedging. And what kind of impact will that hedging have on your corporate performance? The old-school approach answers none of these questions. All it tells you is that you now have 50 percent less risk than you did yesterday.

A CONSERVATIVE HEDGER CHANGES

One of Wayne's first consulting jobs was helping an American energy company that was involved in the production of crude oil and natural gas. They wanted to hedge a recent acquisition so they could guarantee cash flows. When Wayne sat down with senior management, they explained their goal to generate $250 million in revenue from the newly acquired asset during the next two years. Wayne studied their model, which was to hedge ten million barrels of oil, about 75 percent of their production. He immediately spotted a common flaw in the way they were doing the math. They were assuming that the price of oil could go to zero.

"No, no, no, you're looking at this the wrong way," said Wayne. "Oil is currently $25/bbl. It might go down to $18/bbl. over the time horizon you're talking about but never to zero. That means you don't need to hedge ten million barrels of oil. You only need to hedge one million barrels."

Senior management was incredulous. They were skeptical. In their defense, what Wayne was suggesting was radical when compared to the then industry standard. Eventually, they had him meet with the CEO, who understood the math but also had a hard time reconciling it.

"Okay, we're not going to hedge everything," said the CEO. "But you're right. Instead of hedging all of it, we'll just hedge five million barrels. Then we'll monitor it."

"But you only need to hedge a million barrels," replied Wayne.

"No, we're going to hedge five million," the CEO insisted.

> By convincing the firm to reduce the number of hedges, Wayne saved the company $75 million over two years!

So instead of hedging ten million barrels of oil, the firm hedged five million barrels at $25/bbl. And over the life of those hedges, oil prices rose, averaging $40/bbl. By convincing them to reduce the number of hedges, Wayne saved the company $75 million over two years! If they had embraced his advice and hedged just one million barrels, the savings would have been a whopping $135 million.

Managing the Low Case

Senior management was right to be concerned about the potential of the new acquisition to be a negative event in the life of the company. However, they were too conservative in how they were measuring the risk, which would have resulted in their being grossly overhedged if they hadn't asked Wayne to intervene. In this example, more hedges were not needed because prices rose. But if prices had declined, additional hedges might have been called for. Using a hedge process to monitor the firm's risked outcome or Low Case, management could expect alerts whenever the need for more hedges arose should prices have deteriorated. These new hedges would have been at a lower price but still effective at protecting the revenues needed.

You cannot manage the price of a commodity, but you can manage the risked price. If the oil price falls from twenty-five dollars, you can't hedge at twenty-five dollars anymore. But you can still protect your risked price target by adding hedges. The hedges will be at a price lower than twenty-five dollars, and you'll probably have to hedge more volume, but the hedges will still be effective. Adding an appropriate volume of new hedges will adequately protect the firm, so you can continue to assume that it will achieve the budgetary target.

This anecdote is an all-too-common example of what happens when companies use the outmoded approach to risk.

To further illustrate, let's say that a fictional company, W&A Resources, produces ten million barrels of oil each year. W&A Resources decides they want to cut that risk in half. So they lock in the price on half of it. Now what do they have? Well, they have half the risk. How much is that? We don't know. How much did they have before? We don't know that either. Is that number meaningful to them? We just don't know. We don't know any of those things because they never identified how much risk they really had in the first place. We just know that they had risk and by locking in the price, they got rid of half of it.

When communicating with investors, it may be enough to say that W&A Resources is half as risky as another company or as it was. But in terms of financial stability and company sustainability, that action is not necessarily the suitable answer.

For example, W&A Resources projects that its ten million barrels of oil produced per year, with oil currently worth $60/bbl., will generate $600 million per year in revenue. Statistically, it's reasonable to assume that oil prices could fall to $30/bbl., and then W&A might only generate $300 million in revenue. Clearly, W&A has $300 million in risk. Why wouldn't the full $600 million in revenue be at risk? Because, as illustrated in the previous example, oil is likely not going to drop to a value of zero.

So if W&A arbitrarily decided to hedge half of their risk, they essentially reduce their risk to $150 million. That means the projected revenue will have a risked or Low Case of $450 million in revenue. Is that Low Case meaningful to them? They are the only ones who can answer that question. After all, it's their business. One business might say, "No, we need to ensure at least $500 million in revenue because we have a lot of debt." Another business might say, "Actually, $300 million in revenue is just fine because we don't have any debt." By framing risk in this way, we can think of risk in the specific budgetary terms we use to measure success. How to measure risk and manage it is for each company to decide based on their individual needs, goals, and current circumstances.

The key is for W&A to understand how to measure their risk so they can make informed decisions and truly know that how much risk exposure they have is what they can afford to keep.

Instead of hedging to a fixed percentage, wouldn't it be so much more useful to hedge to enterprise performance in order to achieve what the company defines as success?

Hedging Version 1.0: Industry Norm Is to Use a Hedge Percentage

Choosing to consistently hedge a percentage of production will always reduce risk by a proportionate amount. This is often meant to send a clear message to shareholders that you are in this for the long haul and that your strategy is to develop reserves. To illustrate the shortfall of this strategy, consider a firm that hedges 50 percent. They cut the risk in half, but as we pointed out earlier, they don't know if they hedged too much or too little. It might seem like they are in a safe position because they can never be more than 50 percent wrong, and usually much less. Couple this with the realities that the penalty is relatively small for overhedging, because their business will be earning good profits, and the penalty for underhedging is usually small, because the hedges are helping and at least they hedged something. If they always hedge 50 percent, management is going to be okay under most circumstances. However, this strategy appears to be far safer than it is. When extreme adverse price moves occur, which is much more frequently than most people believe, the penalty for underhedging is huge and can be catastrophic. In those moments when a firm should have been 70 percent hedged or more, they often find themselves forced to make huge layoffs, restructure financially, or declare bankruptcy. In short, a strategy to hedge a fixed percentage that is less than 100 percent is playing a form of Russian roulette, which is a very dangerous game. On the other hand, who would hedge everything all the time? No one.

> When extreme adverse price moves occur, which is much more frequently than most people believe, the penalty for underhedging is huge and can be catastrophic.

Hedging Version 2.0: Risked Revenue Clients Manage a Hedge Target

R^2 analytics identifies how much risk there was before and remains after hedging. Hedges are designed to maintain risk at or above specific financial targets that determine a client's success. Risk is "right sized" for each client based on their assets, obligations, and management's risk tolerance. Continued monitoring of Hedge Target(s) allows the client to adjust hedges as market conditions and/ or budgetary estimates change. Risk measured in financial terms and kept within the client's tolerances, as defined by management, will ensure budgetary success under almost any set of circumstances. There is no longer a need to guess how much hedging is needed.

CHALLENGING THE INDUSTRY

The purpose of this book is to place the debate between hedging to a fixed percentage versus hedging to manage enterprise performance out for public consideration. We and our clients have been doing the latter for twenty years. This is your opportunity to carefully consider how this innovative process might help your firm and with it your career.

Hedging a fixed percentage is a lot like filling a car up with gasoline every time your gauge falls to a quarter of a tank. You are always managing to a fixed point, one that you have chosen because it will probably work in most instances. But that technique may not work when conditions experience a radical change and become more acute. Should you get stuck in a traffic jam too long on the way to work, the gas gauge may end up dipping below your threshold. Yet you need to keep going and may not be able to get off the highway to get gas. Despite your quarter-tank plan, you are now risking that you just might run out of gas.

In the winter of 2018 to 2019 in the New York metropolitan area, a snowstorm hit before rush hour, and it took commuters ten hours to get home. Many abandoned their cars when they ran out of gas. If a business made a similar miscalculation, it could result in cash flow shortages that violate debt covenants.

Conversely, you might be taking a long trip on a sparsely populated highway in West Texas. When a gas station appears, you look at your fuel gauge. If you are like most people, you are likely to decide that you really need to fuel up at three-eighths or even half a tank instead of letting it get to a quarter of a tank because there is uncertainty about when the next gas station will be on the horizon. Even better, by looking at a map of gas stations and the range on your dashboard, you'll know exactly how much fuel you'll need. That is Process Risk Management—it improves your chances of consistently achieving your goal and not running out of gas by adapting to your current circumstance. Process focuses on the goal—that is, not running out of gas so you arrive at your destination on time—rather than a rule that allows you to buy gas only when the gauge reads a quarter of a tank.

The foundation of PRM is the idea of risking enterprise performance in a way that hedge decisions are influenced by the market's current price and volatility and all the other moving parts of your business. This is in sharp contrast to hedging a fixed percentage, which is a one-dimensional signpost that will not help you in all circumstances. After assessing risk, the next question for a company to ask is, "What is the threshold of cost or revenue that we need to guarantee?" This is not their budgetary goal, but it is what management has defined as the firm's minimal level or threshold of acceptable performance. Now the firm can place hedges to prioritize and protect the security of that performance threshold, their Hedge Target. The hedges placed with this process protect their budget. It also allows them to "right size" the risk, holding on to all the risk they can afford to keep … which reinforces that *risk is an asset* because they have optimized performance.

A Tale of Two Companies

For a side-by-side comparison, let's examine what happens when Wayne's Old-School Oil Company goes up against Andrew's Innovator Oil. With the old-school approach, Wayne will simply hedge 50 percent of his projected revenue. Since he didn't bother to calculate how much risk he has, his best bet is to split the difference, right? Andrew's Innovator Oil, on the other hand, considers his success metric and ties the hedge decisions to enterprise performance, and he decides to put on enough hedges so that with 95 percent confidence, he will achieve his success metric. To make the comparisons easy, let's say that Andrew's initial hedge also ends up being 50 percent.

With Wayne's company, no matter what happens in or with the market, no changes will be made to the hedge portfolio. In Andrew's case, if prices do nothing but improve, he won't need to consider another hedge. Essentially, with a favorable market move, both firms will be in the same place. Under this scenario, one might say that Andrew did an awful lot of analytical work throughout the year for nothing. Wayne didn't do anything more than place hedges and forget about them. Yet, both ended up in the same place. In this moment, with that one data set and based on the outcome, it would appear Andrew wasted his time and resources. However, Andrew actively monitored the market's impact on his performance and was prepared to adjust his strategy if conditions required him to do so. That didn't occur, and he didn't have to add hedges.

Now let's say that the following year all factors are the same, but prices collapse. Andrew's analytics tell him to put on additional hedges. Prices keep getting lower. Andrew's analysis calls for even more hedges. Prices drop further, and finally Andrew has everything hedged. Under these conditions, Wayne's Old-School Oil Company didn't do a thing to react to the market. He failed to meet budgetary targets, and he may go bankrupt. Andrew's company, on the other hand, remained financially solvent because he reacted to the changing conditions by continuously reigning the risk back to within his firm's tolerance.

In some cases, the results of hedging strategies may look the same because of the stability of the market. But as we have illustrated, the old-school approach can be helpful, but it is not consistently effective. We all have heard that even a broken wristwatch is right twice a day, but who wears a broken watch?

The companies that put their trust in Process Risk Management control their fate and expect to be acceptably healthy *all the time*. They will have the hedges they need when they need them and won't when they don't. They won't have too many hedges when things are going well or too few when things aren't. PRM allows clients to optimize performance through a wide range of price paths over time.

FIGHTING THE LAST BATTLE

As Andrew often says in reference to conventional hedging strategies, "People are always fighting the last battle." Just like a general who would never copy the strategy that the winning side used to secure victory in the previous battle, it's entirely illogical for companies to look at the hedges a successful company placed in the previous year and then follow their lead, expecting it to work again. A good general knows that each battle is different, with a unique set of circumstances, obstacles, and goals.

Yet so often, people try to do things the same way, repeating without thinking what worked for them or others in the past. Even in today's stock market, many analysts are basically looking at an analog for 2000 and 2008 in terms of how those bull markets ended. In truth, the market will not end the way the 2000 or 2008 markets ended. (As this book went to print, the COVID-19 pandemic is likely to be a factor that proves this out.) And because it will end differently, it's critical for companies to stay current, look at the risk they have today, and manage risk based on enterprise performance, as opposed to doing what worked in the past.

A point of clarity is in order here, however. Understanding what happened in the past isn't necessarily foolish. There are lessons to be learned from the past. The philosopher George Santayana famously taught us that "those who don't know history are doomed to repeat it." The past is important, but it's only *part* of today's picture. If you are going to investigate the past at all, understanding *why* a company did what it did is infinitely more useful than memorizing what it did.

And as for the future, we have no idea what's going to happen in the market tomorrow. Nobody does. However, the great thing about PRM is that once a client has helped us understand how much risk is acceptable, we can create a working model to protect it. Then, whenever the market changes adversely and we determine our client has more risk than they can tolerate, we can identify what they should do to be proactive. We have no idea what our path will look like a year from now, but we know that at every turn, we're going to respond appropriately to the risk in that moment.

PRM allows a company to adjust. We don't really care what worked two years ago, because we know that the market is not going to collapse next time like it collapsed last time. However, what we want to know is *when* it's collapsing and *what* we need to do to keep our clients' businesses safe so they can meet their financial goals.

> By hedging to defend enterprise performance, you get the hedges you need, not hedges by rote.

By hedging to defend enterprise performance, you get the hedges you need, not hedges by rote. Need minus rote is over- or under-hedging. When you hedge the minimum requirement for enterprise performance, you have optimized your unhedged risk, making that portion of your risk an asset.

Process Risk Management is an innovation that stands on the shoulders of giants—the giants who developed concepts like the modern portfolio theory, efficient frontier, option pricing models, and other brilliant ideas. For years, companies have been hedging to what amounts to arbitrary volumes, and the limits of that approach have taken a tremendous toll on all, especially on the weaker ones who needed more protection than they thought.

If you have a company to care for, this is a calling for you to start focusing on managing risk to improve enterprise performance. With PRM, you'll be able to establish and maintain 95 percent confidence that you will exceed your budgetary threshold. Producers should remember that you won't be limited to measuring risk in revenues. You can take your calculations to measure the risk to free cash flow or EBITDA. Consumers can measure risk to budgetary targets. Remember that risk is an asset. Mitigate what you must but preserve what you can.

In order to make the most of that risk, you'll have to know how much you have and then you can manage it.

After all, things that get measured, get managed.

Chapter Assets

- Process Risk Management quantifies your risk and allows you to establish risk thresholds or a Hedge Target(s).

- PRM prepares you for and alerts you to actionable events by identifying what, when, how much, and how to hedge.

- You can't protect the Base Case, but you can protect the Low Case.

- By protecting enterprise targets, you will identify attractive opportunities for Market Driven hedges.

- PRM allows you to adjust to changing performance, plans, and conditions.

CHAPTER FOUR

Organizing the Problem and Data

What gets measured, gets managed.

—Peter Drucker

WHEN WE THINK of all the athletes who won the Boston Marathon over the years, or the Olympians who set new world records each season, or Novak Djokovic winning seventeen Grand Slam titles, or Tom Brady taking home six Super Bowl rings, we see tremendous accomplishments captured in a single moment. What we don't see, however, are the endless hours and days and weeks and years of work that went into preparing for that exact moment.

Scoring a touchdown and winning a game is a result of a series of actions and decisions strung together, not simply a single event. We see a pass completion for a touchdown on a Sunday afternoon, and it's easy to think that success was made in that one football throw. In truth, it was composed of the following:

1. Each member spending an entire off-season lifting weights,

maintaining endurance, and stretching

2. A detailed study of the playbook

3. Countless hours of practice between the quarterback and wide receiver to develop precision timing

4. Multiple practice sessions by the eleven-person unit in preparation for the play

5. The proper play called by the offensive coordinator at the appropriate time in the game

6. The wide receiver making the proper decision on the optioned route tree

7. Every offensive lineman holding his block to protect the quarterback

8. The running back picking up a blitz assignment

9. The quarterback delivering the ball to the wide receiver with accuracy

10. The wide receiver catching the ball in stride and evading the defender

A play that looked like it took six seconds on the field in actuality required many months of training and preparation to complete. It is the preparation leading up to such a victory that creates the opportunity for success. As the opening quote for this chapter would suggest, the devil is in the details. The Super Bowl is won on the practice field. Victory is born in

The Super Bowl is won on the practice field.

how each player ties his shoes. It's in the less-than-glorious moments of blocking and tackling. It's in the dozens of procedures that are laborious and mundane. Hall of Famer Michael Strahan summed up his success this way: "The coaches told each of us to do the ordinary. And together, we will be extraordinary."

A SIMPLE MODEL TRANSFORMS UNCERTAINTY INTO AN OPPORTUNITY

Thoreau wrote, "Our life is frittered away by detail ... simplify, simplify."

Indeed, simplification is one mark of real genius. And simplicity is the essence of a market, where all the available information in the world is distilled down to price.

THE ICEBERG ILLUSION
SUCCESS IS AN ICEBERG

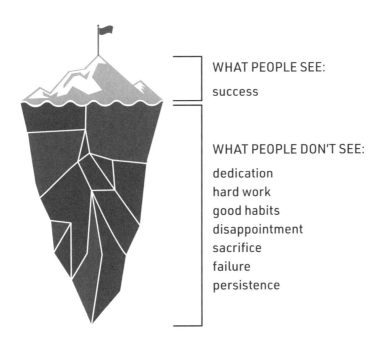

WHAT PEOPLE SEE:

success

WHAT PEOPLE DON'T SEE:

dedication
hard work
good habits
disappointment
sacrifice
failure
persistence

FIGURE 4-1

Success is just the tip of the iceberg, as figure 4-1 illustrates. And the same principles apply to operating a successful business. Corporate leadership must always be mindful of the endless influx of data in order to make informed hedge decisions. Like a Super Bowl win, a successful hedge program relies on a series of decisions, not just a single event. It also requires plenty of preparation and planning. And you can't have an effective plan without securing and properly organizing the data you need.

We all know that markets are volatile and unpredictable. However, we want to give you a mental safety net by explaining that from a hedger's perspective, markets can exhibit just four types of behavior. So before we discuss which data to organize, let's begin with an overview of market behavior and how we'd like you to think about it. All commodities behave erratically, which makes them virtually indistinguishable from each other if you do not know the price. To illustrate our point, the following chart shows multiple price paths for various unrelated commodities at various times in the recent past, including corn, gold, oil, among others. The data was "normalized" by expressing price change as a percentage of each commodity's starting price. Looking at the price paths in this way, it is impossible to identify any of these commodities. Each price path is unique, but collectively these commodities all exhibit similar behavior. This graphic illustrates the range of outcomes we might encounter and want to manage successfully.

PRICE PATHS FOR VARIOUS COMMODITIES

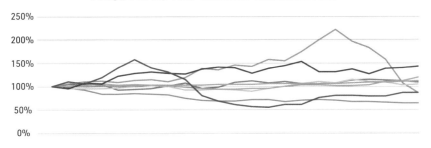

FIGURE 4-2

Let's begin to organize price in the context of the hedge process. Many readers have probably learned about the binomial market model, which assumes that at discrete points in time, there are only two possible outcomes—prices will be either higher or lower. We can use this simple approach, breaking our problem into only two steps, the first of which covers the period when hedges are placed and the second when hedges are settled.

PRICE PATHS FOR VARIOUS COMMODITIES

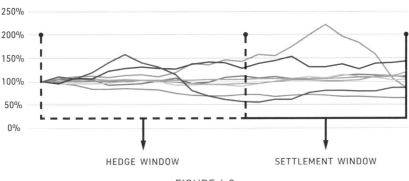

HEDGE WINDOW   SETTLEMENT WINDOW

FIGURE 4-3

Since prices may go up or down in each period, this results in four possible pricing pathways as illustrated in figure 4-4. Just as the binomial models give us a simple idea of how a market might behave, this same concept applies to how PRM can guarantee success.

This simple step allows us to see that each path can be described as one of the four path categories below: up/up, up/down, down/up, or down/down.

FOUR PATHS

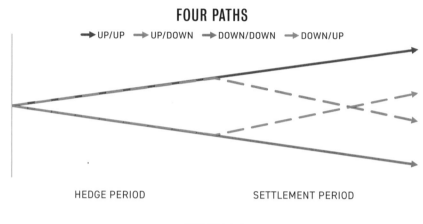

FIGURE 4-4

Looking at this from a producer's perspective, simply put, higher prices are good for producers, and lower prices are not. When prices are going *up*, optimal hedge strategies avoid, delay, and/or minimize hedge activity. In contrast, when prices are going *down*, the reduction in cash flows elevates the need and urgency for hedging. The four price paths and optimal hedge strategy for each may be summarized as follows.

Path Optimal Hedge Strategy for Producers

- up/up: delay or avoid hedging

- up/down: delay but then hedge aggressively

- down/up: hedge but minimize hedge activity

- down/down: hedge early and persistently

If we evaluate the randomness of crude oil and natural gas pricing in this context, we cut through the fog of complexity to find that both markets have exhibited trends but with sharply contrasting behavior patterns. Shown in figure 4-5 are the price paths followed by each commodity since 2007. During this time, crude oil followed an up/up path in six of the nine years. This means that swaps used to hedge were largely, but not consistently, undervalued during the hedge period, because they usually rose to or near the high end of their trading range in the settlement period.

Conversely, natural gas swaps were largely, but not consistently, overvalued throughout the hedge period. In six of the nine years, the price path for gas was either down/down or up/down. Often, gas swaps settled at or near new lows. Except for those who want to hedge away all the risk, PRM is the best way to monitor and manage the resulting enterprise risk exposure, regardless if you are hedging corn, gold, oil, or dirty socks!

> PRM is the best way to monitor and manage the resulting enterprise risk exposure, regardless if you are hedging corn, gold, oil, or dirty socks!

Throughout the study period covered by this analysis, not hedging crude oil would have generally worked well for a producer; that is, with the notable exception of the years 2009 and 2015, when not hedging resulted in producer cash flows shrinking by 30 percent and 45 percent, respectively. In sharp contrast, the most successful hedging strategy for a natural gas producer would have been to hedge early and persistently because gas prices generally fell throughout this study period. Unfortunately, given the importance and random nature of price paths over time, there is no single best strategy.

YEAR	CRUDE OIL					NATURAL GAS				
	HEDGE PER.	SETTLE PER.	START	SETTLE	CHANGE	HEDGE PER.	SETTLE PER.	START	SETTLE	CHANGE
2007	UP	UP	$59.34	$72.34	$13.00	DOWN	DOWN	$9.20	$6.86	$(2.34)
2008	UP	UP	$67.45	$99.65	$32.19	DOWN	UP	$8.69	$9.03	$0.34
2009	UP	DOWN	$88.24	$61.80	$(26.45)	UP	DOWN	$8.17	$3.99	$(4.18)
2010	UP	UP	$63.52	$79.53	$16.01	DOWN	DOWN	$7.74	$4.39	$(3.35)
2011	UP	UP	$79.89	$95.12	$15.23	DOWN	DOWN	$6.41	$4.04	$(2.37)
2012	UP	DOWN	$87.13	$94.20	$7.07	DOWN	DOWN	$5.02	$2.79	$(2.23)
2013	UP	UP	$88.94	$97.97	$9.03	DOWN	UP	$4.37	$3.65	$(0.71)
2014	UP	UP	$92.14	$93.00	$0.86	DOWN	UP	$4.11	$4.41	$0.31
2015	DOWN	DOWN	$88.05	$48.80	$(39.25)	UP	DOWN	$3.87	$2.66	$(1.21)
AVG.			$79.41	$82.49	$3.08			$6.40	$4.65	$(1.75)

FIGURE 4-5

How do you know if prices will go up or down? You can't. Since price can't be predicted, it might seem like a good idea to simply hedge a fixed percentage of volumes ratably by layering into hedges over time. Armed with the information above, one might make the argument that hedging more gas and hedging it earlier than crude oil is a good modification to this strategy. This will comply with historic trends and help achieve an average price in both commodities.

But who would gamble that history will repeat itself when the success of one's business hangs in the balance, especially now that oil and gas prices are well below the high prices seen earlier in the study? A random walk that begins when oil prices are $90/bbl. has completely different budgetary implications than a random walk that begins at $60/bbl. Not to mention those conditions affect a producer much differently than a consumer. Price has a direct impact on profit margins, rendering the economics and risks between these two price examples completely different. Further, one size does not fit all. Should a firm with little debt think about hedging the same way as a firm that is leveraged because it has assumed a lot of debt? Which of these firms has more tolerance for risk and is more likely to survive an adverse price move? If the firm with significant leverage is to have the same level of confidence that its budgetary goals will be achieved, it needs to hedge more than the other, or at least have a plan to cut costs in the event that prices fall.

The goal all businesses share is for another successful year. But how does one manage the vagaries of the markets and business at the same time? How can you build consensus within your firm and create confidence that you have contained risk to an acceptable level? You need a way to monitor conditions and become empowered to respond as necessary to maintain risk within tolerance. That's PRM, but to work it needs data. Let's begin with data.

THE DEVIL IS IN THE DATA

Peter Drucker's "what gets measured, gets managed" quote highlights that one needs to build a foundation by organizing the data properly. The key to organizing data is in what we look at and how we look at it. Whether you are an engineer, a scientist, a risk manager, or anyone making decisions based on numbers, the numbers must be relevant if they are to be useful. With good data that is properly organized in hand, you have a chance to draw reasonable conclusions that will lead to good choices. With bad data or poorly organized data, the information you have is irrelevant, and you'll most likely come to the wrong conclusions.

To begin the process of properly organizing data, we must first assess the range of your possible outcomes. Let's go back to our weather analogy for a moment. If we take, for example, the seasonal average winter temperature in Chicago, it might be fifty degrees colder than the average temperature in the summer. But there's a temperature range even within those winter and summer averages. At the peak of summer, a cold day is probably sixty degrees, and a hot day is probably one hundred degrees. A warm winter day might be fifty degrees, and a cold winter day will likely be below zero.

While the outcomes we expect in January may overlap with the range of outcomes we expect in May, the range of outcomes is dramatically different. We prepare for winter with warmer clothing and for summer with cooler clothing. When we relate this back to organizing data properly, we recognize that the resources we need at our disposal are going to be different as the circumstances change because the range of outcomes we're expecting is different.

What is important to understand here is if we were preparing for a weekend trip to Chicago and simply looked at the annual average temperature, we might end up packing for the hottest possible day and the coldest possible day, which doesn't make any sense. Instead, what do we do? We extract only the data we need and organize it. We consider first the season (summer), then we might look at the month (August), followed by researching the forecast for the days surrounding our trip window. When we drill down, we find ourselves left with only the data that is useful.

We could look at all the data from the last fifty years to see what the weather patterns have been historically. But wouldn't it be more useful to observe what happened in the same month or on the same weekend in history? And how far back should we look? Ten years of data is probably enough; it will give us a good sense of what the range of outcomes is likely to be before we leave. However, if we want to plan for tomorrow's weather, we should look at today's weather because it's probably going to be very similar.

With weather and with hedging, we can, with a high level of confidence, anticipate the range of things that might happen. We can put mechanisms in place that will allow us to do exactly what we want for most of the things in that range. No one can predict what a price will be or what will happen in the market. But we are very good at anticipating the range of things that will happen.

When we consider the universe of things that we can manage, only then are we able to prepare for the universe of things we can't.

> When we consider the universe of things that we can manage, only then are we able to prepare for the universe of things we can't.

The things we can't manage are the things we need insurance for. It's like a tip I was once given on packing for a vacation: Put all the clothes and money you think you'll need for the vacation out on the bed. Then, put half the clothes away and take twice as much money. The money will be your insurance policy.

HOW MUCH DATA IS ENOUGH?

Before you can analyze the data, you must first ask the question, "How much data do we need?" For example, oil prices are available for more than one hundred years, but the fundamentals driving commodity prices today are very different than those just ten years ago. It would be foolish to use data more than ten years old to make a decision about commodity price trends today. In fact, at R^2 we usually limit the data we use to a maximum of one hundred observations, measured in time units relevant to budgetary performances. Since most firms close their books at the end of each month—whether their commodity is priced daily, only on business days, or monthly—we organize the data into a monthly format. Then we use a minimum of thirty-six months and a maximum of one hundred. This has served us well.

The book *Chaos and Order in the Capital Markets* by Edgar E. Peters was among the first to apply chaos theory to the world of finance, repudiating the "random walk" theory and econometrics in favor of a more general view of the forces influencing the capital market system. In the decades following its publication, Peters's book has become the industry gold standard to which analysts, investors, and traders turn for a comprehensive overview of chaos theory. That said, when organizing data, Edgar Peters recommends using between 30 and 120 data points. Less than 30 and you will not have a representative sample. More than 120 and you have noise, which prevents you from seeing how underlying forces are affecting the market.

THE MONTHLY MODEL

As stated earlier in this chapter, most businesses close their accounting books each month. To coordinate their hedge programs with accounting, their data analysis should dovetail this time frame by using a monthly yardstick. We recommend using three to four years of monthly data because, in most instances, it will identify current trends but will be responsive to trend changes.

Let's explore the question, "How much monthly data is important?" a little deeper. Technological innovations and consumer preferences work in time cycles much less than ten years. So ten years of data is likely going to provide you with an unrepresentative average.

Figure 4-6 is a monthly bar graph for gold prices with the average for three, five, ten, and twenty years shown. The three- and five-year averages are colored green because we believe these sets hold the most relevant data for strategic decision making. It appears that the ten-year data provides an equally good estimate. However, with 120 months of data, the average will be slow to change as new economic factors affect gold prices. And consider that the price range over ten years is twice what it has been for the past three years. To fully appreciate this point, the twenty-year data set has a range twice again that of the ten-year and an average price that is 30 percent lower than the other three, because it still includes gold prices as low as $258 per ounce. We want the data we use to represent *today's* market and its potential. What happened ten or twenty years ago is no longer relevant to today's economics.

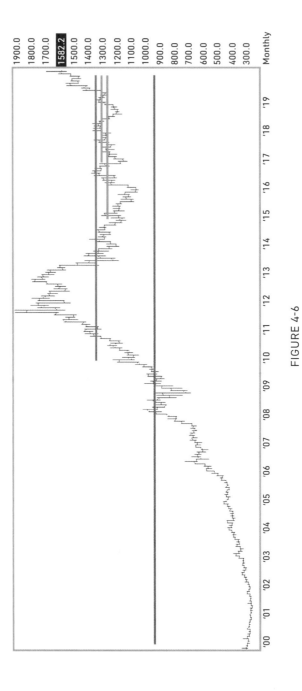

FIGURE 4-6

Also notice the transitions from one price trend/environment to another, such as can be seen in late 2011 when gold peaked at ~$1,900. Price reversals are often abrupt and usually persistent. It may not seem helpful, but it is important to appreciate that markets, when viewed as a chaotic system, can be described as having a high probability for behaving one way, until that abruptly changes. Then there is a high probability of it behaving in a new and consistently different way.

Given this, everyone should expect the market to behave tomorrow like it did today, and that's a very reasonable expectation. What no one can see coming is when the market is about to make another paradigm shift. Those are moments when a market goes from the old normal to a *new* normal. It is impossible to predict when that's going to happen or what the new normal will be. But PRM—our methodical, process-driven approach—will prepare you for and identify the adjustment(s) needed to assure minimum budgetary goals are being met. PRM will alert you before your firm is in jeopardy.

Importantly, PRM analytics allow you to respond to risk even before trend changes can be identified. When consumers manage risk to a key performance metric by maintaining the High Case below target or the low-water mark of the High Case, they will, in fact, be proactively responding to new developments in the market. Similarly, producers who maintain the Low Case above their financial target or maintain the high-water mark of the Low Case will also respond to market developments and keep their firm out of harm's way.

Responding on a monthly time frame is usually frequent enough to be responsive to market changes, and it avoids reacting to temporary blips in pricing that reflect noise rather than trends. However, any time you are close to your risk threshold and prices jump, it may be prudent to update your risk map midmonth. You won't get it right all the time. No one can. But take solace knowing that if you do hedge and these hedge adjustments are not accompanied by a new trend, then you will have just a few poorly placed hedges that should have little impact on your overall budgetary performance. On the other hand, if prices persist negatively, then these hedges are likely to provide some of the protection needed to achieve success.

HOW TO USE DATA

It is convenient to assume that successful people in business had a lucky break or moment of brilliance. The reality is that success is usually built in small steps using rigorous discipline that adheres to driving principles. It is the consistency that eventually pays off in success.

How many times a year should a CFO be looking at commodity prices in order to decide on hedging? Two hundred and fifty times (daily)? Fifty-two times (weekly)? Twelve times (monthly)? Or one time (annually)? Managing decisions with monthly updates to data enables businesses to respond proactively to meaningful changes in price. If businesses are responding to daily or even weekly data, it may take time away and distract them from their core competencies. At the other extreme, if they respond to price just once or twice per year, they may not be nimble enough to protect themselves from significant price moves. Our recommendation is to monitor weekly price updates, and unless prices make a large move, limit hedge decisions to those identified with monthly enterprise updates.

As Tony Robbins says, "Successful people aren't those who made the fewest mistakes, but those who made the most." The bottom line: break your decisions into a series of small steps and be ready to adjust or reinvent your strategy as necessary.

Here is one example of how we analyzed data for a client who wanted to review their process. This happened to be a large petroleum consumer client who was a systematic purchaser of refined product. We were tasked to find a more cost-effective way for them to make fuel purchases. We looked back at the daily data for the past 120 months, looking for a pattern within the calendar month that might be helpful. The data revealed that if they bought during a specific window of each month, the pricing on average would be advantageous.

Next we had to design a test to see if the data was misleading or the trends changing. We divided the data into subsets; for example, splitting the sample up into three separate forty-eight-month periods to verify the consistency of our observation across all data subsets. We also analyzed each year as a stream of continuous twelve-month periods. No matter how we divided the data into subsets, our original conclusion remained valid. Each subset of the data exhibited the same pattern. The differences were small and could have been easily overlooked, but they were significant. We had found an opportunity. What we did differently was to observe the price paths within each month to determine when we were most likely to establish the high and low any month. We expected these to occur randomly, but they exhibited a pattern that was consistent from month to month. Then we dug deeper, examining who the market participants were and how they behaved. We wanted to understand why this opportunity existed. In the end, the customer confirmed what we learned and made a strategic modification to their buying patterns. This gave them a meaningful edge that translated into an eight-figure average fuel cost reduction per year.

Before the study, we would have guessed what everyone else

believed: that systematic buying would achieve the average. The math is simple: whether you buy each day or every Friday or every third day, you are random sampling, in which you should expect to achieve the average over time. What we learned about this market is that buyers are aggressive near month end because they want to close their monthly books. Conversely, buyers are temporarily absent a few days into the month, probably because they have time to buy and other responsibilities take priority. Throughout this ten-year period, regardless if prices were near their highs or lows, prices were measurably higher at the end of each month than they were at the beginning. Our client simply bought more when there was less competition, early in the month.

We were able to identify that this strategy could add value because we looked at it differently. While the benchmark was the monthly average, evaluating the daily data for this market revealed that it had a pattern or tell—one that our client, because of their unique position in the industry, could exploit.

What was the risk of changing their buying process? Most likely that the edge would disappear, and prices would become random throughout the month. That would not hurt the client. But to look for that and make sure that a new pattern did not evolve, continued monitoring of the data using thirty-six to forty-eight months of results should be enough to find changes if and when they develop.

In the bigger picture, please consider the following:

- Risk is an asset: In this case the consumer was perpetually short. The consumer had to buy but never needed to sell. They only had to confront half the problem that traders, who must buy lower than they sell, are faced with. As long as this consumer bought below the average, they had an edge on the competition. That goal is achievable most of the time.

- In any one single year, the strategy does not have to work. If the strategy is consistently applied over many years, we would expect it will bear out. Importantly, the strategy won't work every month. In months when you buy early and prices fall dramatically, you will not beat the average. To capture this edge, you will need patience and deep pockets.

- Monetizing this advantage as a trader is almost impossible, because the margins are small, and the volatility is large. Monetizing this advantage for a small asset holder is difficult, because they typically won't be in the market every month. Assuming they are in the market on random months, at best it will take more time to accumulate enough random months to develop a representative sample. Because traders and small asset holders won't bother, this statistical advantage remained viable for and important to the larger asset holder.

Chapter Assets

- Markets are complex, but all follow one of four paths.
- Paths cannot be predicted but can be managed.
- For most business problems, 30–120 monthly data observations are appropriate.
- If the data covers less than three years, use weekly data.

CHAPTER FIVE

Quantifying Risk

We can all create our own luck by taking the necessary risks
to open the door of change, progression, and success.

—Peter Branson

IF YOUR SPOUSE ASKS you to stop at the supermarket and bring home dinner, how much meat do you buy? It would be helpful to know how many people you are cooking for. What are their ages? An eighteen-year-old male will likely eat twice as much as another adult. Together with an accurate head count and a rough approximation of half a pound per person, you'll get it right. But what if there might be more people coming? There will be a risk of not having enough food for everyone. To be confident you've bought enough meat, you must assess the likelihood that more people will arrive and how many might actually show up. By quantifying the risk of how many more pounds of meat may be eaten, you can make a better decision on how much food to buy.

Each day, people make quantified assessments of risk and choose how to live their lives. For instance, some people won't go in the water at the beach because they are concerned about the risk of sharks. Yet there are many life-forms that put us at an even greater risk. Let's quantify that based on a 2018 study.

Number of people worldwide who die from the following, per year:[2]

- Sharks: 6

- Wolves: 10

- Lions: 22

- Elephants: 500

- Hippopotamuses: 500

- Tapeworms: 700

- Crocodiles: 1,000

- Roundworms: 4,500

- Mosquitos: 750,000

By quantifying data, we can ascertain the true risk as opposed to the *perceived* risk. In this example, by using historical data we can glean the relative risk, holding other conditions constant. Can the data always be taken at face value? Considering that many of the risks above are native to the continent of Africa, a shark in the water when you are visiting a US beach would still hold more risk to you than a mosquito (due to lack of malaria or West Nile virus). In absolute terms, the risks from a shark would be highly unlikely unless mitigated by other factors.

Yet many businesses make critical decisions without collecting

---

2   Lydia Ramsey, "These Are the Top 15 Deadliest Animals on Earth," Science Alert, accessed February 24, 2020, https://www.sciencealert.com/what-are-the-worlds-15-deadliest-animals.

and measuring the data in terms of risk as it relates to their goals. "How much should I hedge? Should I hedge at all?" At its core, quantifying risk relies on models of probability and game theory—that is, mathematical models that study interactions among rational decision makers and how their strategic decisions affect the overall outcome.

Essentially, quantifying risk comes down to understanding and anticipating how things may play out. But how do you model that?

> At its core, quantifying risk relies on models of probability and game theory—that is, mathematical models that study interactions among rational decision makers and how their strategic decisions affect the overall outcome.

THE MARKET PROVIDES AN IMPLIED RANGE OF PRICES

The risking of prices is an essential building block for our risk assessments. To risk price, we need an accurate estimate of the market's volatility. There are many ways to measure a market's volatility, which are arguably all accurate. We wanted one that is not only objective but that reflects the current thinking of those closest to the industry. To understand why we prefer our methodology, first you need to understand where trading started. The first transaction was probably as simple as one party needing cash today and the other party thinking the traded item would be worth more sometime in the future. The buyer might have had information that they believed was either of better quality or that they got earlier than everybody else and wanted to use this for their gain. To capitalize on this information, the buyer found other people to trade with, which eventually led to the development of a market with lots of trading activity.

Much later, options were introduced. They filled the need for those who needed to know they could buy or sell something but were not in a position to do it now. How options are priced is a key element to understanding why Process Risk Management is so effective. While there is a litany of option pricing models available today, they all took their lead from traders who priced options before any of the models were developed. How did stock traders agree on the price of the first option? It probably began when something like this happened: someone owned a stock priced at thirty dollars (the underlying instrument) and a trader wanted the right to buy the stock (a call option) at thirty dollars.

How did these two decide what that option was worth? To answer this question, we must calculate what the option payout will be over an estimated range of likely prices. It is this payout profile that will determine how the option should be priced. This simplified example will help you to appreciate how traders priced the first options. More importantly, understanding which factors were relevant to their calculations made it possible for all option pricing models and PRM to be developed.

Most traders today are too young to appreciate that all option pricing models were developed to mimic what traders had been doing for years. They might wonder, "How is it possible to calculate an option's value in your head?" Consider, for example, the stock that is currently trading for thirty dollars a share (underlying price), which has a trading range of twenty dollars to forty dollars (volatility element). If you bought the stock, your expectation would be that it can go up or down ten dollars a share. But what would a thirty-dollar (strike price) call option be worth? (Calls give you the right, but not the obligation, to buy at a specific price.) That's what traders figured out, and eventually some very bright people like Black and

Scholes developed option pricing models. To keep the math simple, let's assume at option expiration (time element) that the stock will be randomly one of five prices: twenty dollars, twenty-five dollars, thirty dollars, thirty-five dollars, or forty dollars. Ignoring the cost of the thirty-dollar call option for now, its payout would look like the following:

$20 = 0
$25 = 0
$30 = 0
$35 = $5
$40 = $10

Buying that option for free would be a great deal, because you could make five dollars or ten dollars with no chance of losing anything. But who would sell it to you for free? No one. The more important question is, "How much would I be willing to pay for it?" Since each outcome has a one-fifth or 20 percent chance of occurring, the expected value of these payouts is one-fifth of the total possible payouts: ($0 + $0 +$0 +$5 + $10 = $15)/5, or three dollars. Coincidentally, that is what the option is worth. If you paid three dollars each time you bought the option and you did that five times, you would have paid fifteen dollars in total for the five options. Then, provided that you got an average of the random expiration price outcomes, you'd break even. Buy the option for less than three dollars, and you should expect to make money. Pay more, expect to lose.

Now, the real world is much more complicated. First, we can't limit ourselves to five price outcomes. To value an option, you must do the math for every possible price outcome. Option models conveniently do that for us. What the option is worth is the information most traders are interested in. As asset managers, the price of an option tells us something else that is very important. The price of the option itself provides us with an excellent estimate for how much the price of a commodity is expected to move.

We use the traded price of an option to calculate the implied price range of the underlying instrument. The key advantage is that instead of observing prices of the underlying stock or commodity to calculate its mean and standard deviation (SD), which gives us one estimate, using options provides us with an estimate that represents a consensus of all market participants. By reversing the math, we can use option prices to observe the range that traders expect for the stock or commodity. In this case, if we see that the option for a thirty-dollar call on a thirty-dollar stock is worth three dollars, we conclude that the expected range for the stock is twenty dollars to forty dollars.

> We use option prices to observe the price range that traders expect for a stock or commodity.

If the call was one dollar, we'd expect the range to be approximately 27-33 dollars.

We use option prices to observe the price range that traders expect for a stock or commodity. This volatility estimate is unique because it is determined by consensus. It is objective, impartial, and can be updated every day. We observed that when it came to hedging, it appeared that no one had ever used a volatility estimate determined by consensus to develop an expected price range for commodities. Further, no one appreciated that once management had an objective assessment of price potential, it would be in a better position to prepare for and manage risk. Stated simply, using a volatility estimate determined by consensus allows a business to objectively assess what it will look like throughout a range of prices. It is letting "the market" tell you what can happen.

MONTE CARLO FORECASTING

When companies are thinking about their hedging, during the period of time when they are trying to reduce risk, prices can do one of two things, as described in the previous chapter: they can go up or down. During the time that their risk strategy is in place, prices can also do one of two things: they can go up or down. At a very basic level, that leaves four possible paths: prices can go up while they're hedging and up while they're settling; up while they're hedging and down while they're settling; down while they're hedging and then bounce back up when they're settling; or down when they're hedging and down when they're settling.

The active period is the hedge window, when company leadership acknowledges that they have too much risk and are committed to managing it. PRM analytics provide leadership with guidance to manage the path over time. Risk assessments are made throughout both windows. It doesn't only happen at three focal points—the hedge window, when it switches from the hedge window to the settlement period, and then when the settlement is complete. There's a serpentine path that begins before the start of the hedge window and continues through to settlement. The key to effectively managing this path is understanding what the path might look like. Monte Carlo simulations are used to estimate the risk at each step along the way.

If, for example, you only have a single commodity, your risk profile could be modeled using a log normal distribution. Log normal distributions are a bit like a bell-shaped curve, but they do not let the price fall below zero. This barrier allows them to better represent assets, because assets cannot be worth a negative amount without becoming a liability. However, all you have calculated is what the range of outcomes might be. You have no insight into the possible pathway the price can follow. For asset managers, it is not enough to know where you will end up. They need to understand the path—how good or bad things might get along the way—to be fully prepared for the challenges they may face. Monte Carlo simulations provide that information.

More importantly, when you have two or more commodities at risk, like crude and natural gas, you simply must use Monte Carlo simulations. Risk assessments for multiple commodities will over-estimate the risk if we simply add the results together, because the chance of both or all of them going to either their lows or their highs at the same time is very small. Monte Carlo simulations are the only way to estimate all the things that may happen and are essential when you have multiple asset classes.

GAUSSIAN PROBABILITY DISTRIBUTION VS. MONTE CARLO SIMULATION

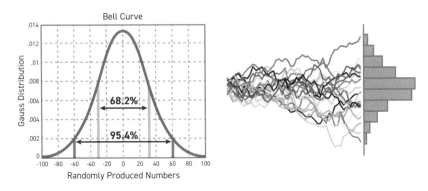

FIGURE 5-1

The strength of Monte Carlo models is that they can model complex systems and can also simultaneously model multiple probability distributions. This allows us to put conditions on the distribution that you can't with a Gaussian distribution.

Let's say that today oil is $50/bbl. and we know that in two years it could be as high as $90/bbl. or as low as $25/bbl. That's not a very helpful piece of information. Monte Carlo simulations are used to provide simulated pathways for that two-year period, building them one month at a time. For example, if you take today's price and risk it for one month, you will get a new random price, perhaps $52/bbl. Then if you proceed to the next month, risking that fifty-two-dollar price will generate a new price that might be higher or lower. Continue to repeat this process for each month through to settlement and you will generate one possible price path. For our work, each data point is risked for a relatively short period of time—one month. Monte Carlo simulations allow us to build paths in which, like the real world, each price observation along the path is impacted by all the points that precede it in the path.

Individually, each of these paths is not likely to tell us much because they were randomly generated. But as a group they can be expected to equally represent each of the four path categories discussed earlier. That's why we repeat this process to generate a sample set of paths. By running this simulation hundreds or thousands of times, you get a distribution of possible outcomes that accurately reflects what could happen in the real world.

For our clients, we look at the sampling of paths generated and eliminate the top 5 percent and bottom 5 percent of outcomes to create the 90 percent confidence interval. This data is shown by year as a box plot in figure 5-2. And then we use the same process where we eliminate the top 25 percent of outcomes and the bottom 25 percent of outcomes to create the 50 percent confidence interval, and we're left with the dark-shaded area in the box plots. Since we allow each commodity to follow its own path and then sum up the results, Monte Carlo allows for the noncorrelation component between commodities; that is, that they are unlikely to both be at their highs or lows together.

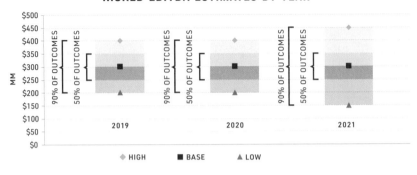

FIGURE 5-2

Elements of game theory abound in discussing strategic decisions and forecasting the future of commodities. One key assumption needed to model price potential is volatility. As we briefly discussed earlier in this chapter, there are an infinite number of ways to measure it, and it is impossible to prove that one method is more accurate than another. To manage this dilemma, R^2 uses option pricing data to determine which volatilities to use in its Monte Carlo simulations. This is very important, so we will deliberately repeat ourselves: embedded in an option price is an assumption about the market's volatility. We can reverse engineer from the settlement price of an option what volatility must have been used to determine that price. More importantly, since the option price used is its published settlement, its value and the assumptions used to determine it represent a consensus of all market participants. This is truly an objective assessment of volatility, one that reflects the current expectation of traders for the magnitude of likely market moves.

As new prices and volatilities are observed, we use algorithms or a series of mathematical calculations to update our model inputs on a regular basis. Then by rerunning risk reports, we can monitor how the dynamics of changing market conditions and hedge actions have impacted our client's risk. The value brought to clients by PRM is the creation of a feedback loop that uses market data to provide objective observations about their risk exposures.

THE POWER OF A FEEDBACK LOOP

When a new restaurant is launched, there is always a learning curve for management as they develop an understanding for how much of each specific food should be on hand at any given time. In the opening weeks, there may be a lot of waste or even shortages of menu items. Managing food supplies is a dynamic problem. On holidays and weekends, customers typically will make different requests for their products than, say, on a weekday at noon. And the restaurant can expect to experience seasonal preferences. Perhaps they'll sell more burgers in the summer and beef stew in the winter. To be successful, the new restaurant must use a feedback loop to adapt to the constantly changing desires of their clientele. If they do that, they will end up getting better and better until at last their projections are extremely accurate and remain current.

The only constant is change. When quantifying the data, you just can't take one snapshot and walk away. The power of PRM is in updating data and retesting your assumptions one month later and then two months later and then three months later and so on. By monitoring changing conditions, you will adapt to each new environment and maintain performance.

PRECISION vs. ACCURACY

BOTH ESTIMATES ARE PRECISE, BUT ONLY ONE IS ACCURATE.

FIGURE 5-3

Now, you may have wondered, "If we are making assumptions about volatility, how accurate are our estimates?" It's time to have a short discussion about the difference between precision and accuracy. Frankly, we know these objective risk estimations are not 100 percent accurate. The table below provides the results of a study where the 50 percent and 90 percent confidence intervals were back tested. If these estimates were accurate, we would expect them to contain 50 percent and 90 percent of the outcomes, respectively. Instead, we were met with the following results:

HISTORICAL OBSERVATION SUMMARY

In contrast to the forward curve not being a strong predictor of future prices, implied volatilities of NG and WTI options have been generally strong predictors of future volatility 12 months out.

NG (#, % OF MONTHLY SETTLES)	1–12 MO	13–24 MO	25–36 MO
LQ-HQ (50% expected)	1,079 (50%)	734 (36%)	461 (25%)
LOW-HIGH (90% expected)	1,889 (87%)	1,612 (80%)	1,460 (78%)
> HIGH (5% expected)	72 (3%)	69 (3%)	88 (5%)
< LOW (5% expected)	205 (9%)	341 (17%)	330 (18%)
TOTAL	2,166 (100%)	2,022 (100%)	1,878 (100%)

WTI Swap (#, % OF MONTHLY SETTLES)	1–12 MO	13–24 MO	25–36 MO
LQ-HQ (50% expected)	1,013 (47%)	839 (41%)	701 (37%)
LOW-HIGH (90% expected)	1,804 (83%)	1,388 (69%)	1,136 (60%)
> HIGH (5% expected)	144 (7%)	384 (19%)	487 (26%)
< LOW (5% expected)	218 (10%)	250 (12%)	255 (14%)
TOTAL	2,166 (100%)	2,022 (100%)	1,878 (100%)

Further out than 12 months, settlements have breached their 50% and 90% risk bands more frequently than expected.

FIGURE 5-4

As an example, for WTI crude oil in the one- to twelve-month horizon, we remained in the band of the High to Low Case (90 percent expected) 83 percent of the time. It was 87 percent for gas. Pretty good, but not perfect. Next, look at what happened in the two- and three-year time horizons. When forecasting for those longer periods, the estimates of risk were *not* high enough! The High to Low Case only occurred ~60–80 percent of the time, not 90 percent of the time.

The confidence estimates we calculate are good estimates, based on the best information available at the time. They are precise but probably not accurate. That is why *process* is so important. It doesn't matter if you know accurately whether you have 95 percent or 85 percent confidence. It may affect how much you hedge but not the outcome. Remember that we can't defend a price, but we can defend a risked price. That means we can protect a risked performance threshold.

For asset managers this becomes increasingly important over time and a powerful tool. The risked estimates are precise because they get used repeatedly without a change in the methodology. They are also actionable because the business can use the information provided to employ a process to hedge to their target. Whether or not the confidence interval is accurate, if hedges are added whenever risk exceeds your tolerance as defined by your target, you can expect to achieve or beat the target. If you hedge to protect a target, you can expect to achieve the target.

Businesses are not typically budgeting/planning aggressively three years out. For periods where management has yet to identify a Hedge Target, they can still manage risk. Producers can defend as their target the high-water mark of their Low Case. Conversely, consumers can defend the low-water mark of their High Case.

PRECISION vs. ACCURACY

INCREASING THE TIME FOR ANY ESTIMATE DECREASES ITS ACCURACY.

FIGURE 5-5

Chapter Assets

- Options provide price potential estimates determined by a consensus of market participants.

- Monte Carlo simulations are used to estimate risk because the path is important.

- Precise risk estimates are effective whether or not they are accurate, as long as they are regularly updated.

CHAPTER SIX

PRM Using Success Metrics

It's not what we do once in a while that shapes
our lives. It's what we do consistently.

—Tony Robbins

HOW DOES A PROFESSIONAL sports team measure success? Is it with ticket sales? Is it by reaching the playoffs? Or is there only one measure of success—winning the championship? There are clearly some sports organizations that hire and instruct personnel based on many or all the above and yet that might provide conflicting directives in achieving those goals. Achieving the first two would be more likely if the team acquired a well-known football star who would generate ticket sales and ultimately provide the team with a resource that could put it in a better position to make the playoffs. But that player would be expensive and impact the team's salary cap (using up a large percentage of the amount of money allocated to all players), thereby making it more difficult to attract other talented players and assemble a robust team capable of winning a championship.

Businesses are similar in that they may have conflicting strategic objectives. Organizations communicate goals to their stakeholders that are unique to each company. One public company may attract investors because they are making a commitment to generate dividends. Another business might emphasize growth. Some of these use leverage. Because they are holding a lot of debt, they need robust cash flow to generate enough EBITDA for them to maintain the debt/EBITDA ratios needed to satisfy their debt covenants.

> Defining success is critical in any endeavor, because without something to measure, how will you know when you have achieved your goals?

Defining success is critical in any endeavor, because without something to measure, how will you know when you have achieved your goals? It sounds simple and may seem obvious, but many businesses fail to properly define what success looks like or are using the wrong metric to measure it.

COMMON METRICS FOR PRODUCER SUCCESS

- Revenue
- Free cash flow
- EBITDA
- Debt/EBITDA
- IRR
- Payment of dividend

COMMON METRICS FOR CONSUMER SUCCESS

- Cost
- Percent of budget
- Budget ceiling
- Customer delivered rate (ratepayer tariff, no airline ticket fuel surcharge)
- Payment of dividend

A popular industry term used to help organizations maintain their own success is business process management (BPM). BPM is a discipline in operations *management* in which people use various methods to discover, model, analyze, measure, improve, optimize, and automate *business processes*. Applied to project *management*, business *process management* is the use of a repeatable *process* to maximize the outcome of the project by minimizing inefficiencies. Process Risk Management echoes this, but because it is applied to an uncertain world, rather than focusing on maximizing outcomes, it seeks to optimize performance. Put another way, rather than seeking to make the most money at the risk of losing everything, PRM seeks to make money consistently and avoid any chance of bankruptcy. In each of these models, the key to success is to align the organization's processes and the metrics it uses with its strategic goal(s).

The first step is to avoid measuring the wrong or superfluous things and to identify the metrics that drive your success!

BUSINESS PROCESS MANAGEMENT LIFE CYCLE

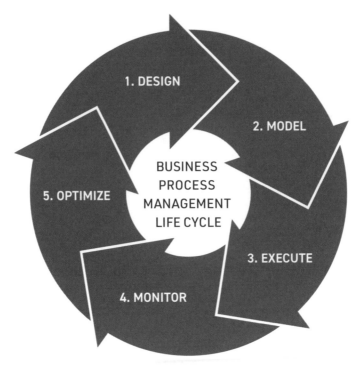

FIGURE 6-1

Talking specifically about hedging, identifying and sticking to a particular percentage of risk to be hedged is not a metric that supports strategic goals; it simply describes the firm's relative exposure to price. In PRM, companies measure financial indicators that *drive* success, things like revenue, free cash flow, EBITDA, and debt/EBITDA ratios among others.

Next, you build a model of the company that will generate stressed estimates of the success metric(s). The model will have three categories of inputs: (1) the volumes that your firm expects it will consume and/or produce, (2) the hedges it currently has in place, and (3) market pricing data plus risked estimates of that data. Volumes are multiplied by an array of prices to calculate their cost or value under current and risked pricing conditions. These volumes and price inputs are combined by the model to generate performance estimates. The model's output must be in units that management uses to gauge its own performance—that is, the metric that identifies whether it achieved success.

These estimates should be recorded and tracked over time because both the notional value and relative changes in these values are important. Success is relative. Success is meeting a minimum performance level for a specific set of financial goals that are relevant to your company. But first, the goals must be clearly defined.

> The model's output must be in units that management uses to gauge its own performance—that is, the metric that identifies whether it achieved success.

SUCCESS IS RELATIVE; MAXIMIZE OR OPTIMIZE

Let's use the example of two up-and-coming professionals, Jane and Doug. They have similar incomes and live in the same neighborhood. Both have families with young dependents, and each one is the primary income earner responsible for the needs of their family. On the surface we might expect that the two have equal success, but that is not the case. Each has their individual priorities and, consequently, employs a different strategy to achieve that goal.

Both young professionals statistically are at a very low risk of being disabled or passing early. And neither does. Yet Jane chooses to spend thousands of dollars per year on disability insurance and life insurance, while Doug does not. Doug has better bottom-line performance because he avoided paying insurance premiums, but is he truly more successful?

To reiterate, success is defined by reaching and/or exceeding minimum stated goals. Both Doug and Jane defended a minimum cash flow target, and each was successful. If the goal is maximum bottom-line performance, then Doug achieved success. But he did so by consciously forgoing the cost/benefit of insurance, leaving his family in a riskier position than Jane's. All it would take to upend Doug's life is a catastrophic event, and suddenly he and his family would be facing financial ruin. On the other hand, if the goal is to provide for the needs of the family under any set of circumstances, Jane is more successful. Rather than maximize, her strategy was to *optimize* performance. Jane has certainly done that and will provide for her family's needs because insurance, whether it is a disability policy or a targeted hedge plan, minimizes or removes the luck variable by managing the risk of those negative outcomes.

Therein lies the reason people are confused about traditional risk management—it appears to work … *some* of the time. As long as Doug is not disabled, Jane's hedge program looks like an unnecessary cost center. If we consider a 50 percent hedge program, it is easy to imagine that this may be enough for most companies under average market conditions. Yet as soon as the market behavior is exaggerated, things can go wrong very fast, and the view of what is adequate will change. Eventually, extreme adverse price conditions will occur, and then it won't matter whether you hit your goals for a few years when, because of one market event, you are out of business and no longer able to stay in the game. Rather than hedge a percentage of volumes, it is more important to quantify your risk and then reduce and maintain it at acceptable levels.

MONITORING THE METRICS OF SUCCESS

The world will change, and prices will change. The impact these may have on your firm might determine if it exceeds or falls behind on its performance targets. When changes are significant, adjustments may be necessary to ensure the success of those targets, as the following examples illustrate.

Imagine that the graphic in figure 6-2 represents a minimum financial target of the EBITDA for an oil producer, P&F Industries, set at $200 million. Senior leadership has determined that that number defines their success and allows them to achieve their goals. As shown, we can see that the company is 95 percent confident its EBITDA will exceed $150 million and 75 percent confident it will exceed $250 million.

FIGURE 6-2

Now, if we hedge enough to remove $50 million of risk, it will shrink the 50 percent and 90 percent confidence intervals, as seen in figure 6-3. More importantly, we're going to raise the Low Case to the firm's minimum target, giving them 95 percent confidence of success. In doing so, the company gave up something on the upside, as the High Case dropped from $450 million down to $400 million.

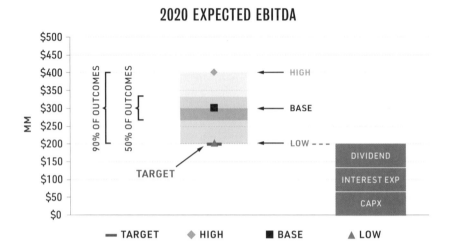

Hedge decisions manage both upside potential and downside risk. Risk is monitored so targets can be protected as prices change.

FIGURE 6-3

Confidence intervals, unlike percentage hedged, give you a way of describing how much risk you are willing to hold. You can't say you hedged to a 95 percent confidence level without saying confidence in *what*. Without a hedge this firm was 95 percent confident EBITDA would exceed $150 million, and 75 percent confident that EBITDA would exceed $250 million. The second EBITDA reference amount is higher, but now there is a 25 percent chance you won't achieve it. There is a 20 percent chance EBITDA will be between $150 and $250 million and a 5 percent chance it will be below $150 million.

Are these confidence estimates accurate? As we discussed in the previous chapter, they are good estimates, but beyond Year 1 they are probably not accurate. And as we discussed, these estimates will change over time. This is why *process* is so important. It really does not matter if you are 95 percent or 85 percent confident. That affects when and how much you hedge, not the outcome. Whether or not the confidence interval is an accurate descriptor, if hedges are added whenever the Low Case falls below target, one can expect the target to be achieved. Managing to a risked target regardless of confidence interval, combined with using a consistent process, turns a precise estimate of risk into a dependable and successful defense of that performance target.

To see this in operation over time, let's take a similar company and instead use revenue as the metric of success. Assuming the firm has a million barrels of production each year, with oil trading $66/bbl., the Base Case estimate for revenue is $66 million. When we risk the oil price down statistically, we get $42/bbl., which would translate into a Low Case revenue estimate of $42 million. If this firm needed to generate at least $54 million, that would be their Hedge Target. Based on the assumptions provided, it is easy to calculate that they need to hedge 50 percent of their production (0.5 million bbl. × $66/bbl. + 0.05 million bbl. × $42/bbl. = $54 million). If the Hedge Target was $48 million, then they would need to hedge 25 percent of production at this time to ensure success.

EXAMPLE: HEDGE TARGET OF $54 FOR 2008

In 2008 hedges that reduced risk by 50% targeted a WASP of $54/bbl. As prices rose, analytics confirmed that additional hedges were not required because risk estimates remained above the **"Hedge Target."** Higher prices lifted the WASP to $82.46/bbl.

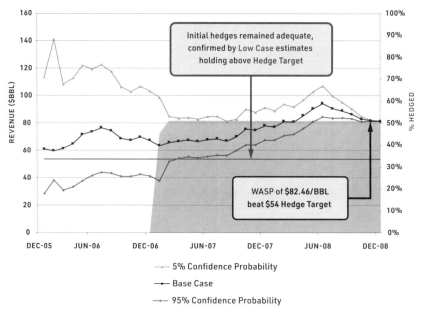

In strong markets, **overhedging can be avoided** with R^2 analytics.

FIGURE 6-4

The blue shaded area (figure 6-4) indicates that they put on a 50 percent hedge, which is the metric along the vertical axis to the right. By doing that, the Low Case (red line) was lifted to the $54 million in Hedge Target (purple line). In this case, the Base Case (black line) kept rising after the hedge because prices just kept getting better. Note also that the Low Case kept improving as well. Once the hedges were placed, it remained at or above the Hedge Target, so there was never any reason to add more hedges. If the Low Case in this example had fallen below the Hedge Target, then adding more hedges would have been recommended to lift the Low Case back up above the Hedge Target.

Let's look at another time period to see how hedges would be added in a price environment that got worse. Notice in figure 6-5, in this higher-priced environment, that the firm's new Hedge Target is $75/bbl. or revenues of $75 million. Again, the blue shaded area initially jumps to 50 percent as the initial hedges are added. This lifted the Low Case to the Hedge Target, where it stayed at or above for several months. When prices eventually fell enough to take the Low Case below the Hedge Target, additional hedges were added. This occurred on four separate occasions. Specifically, each hedge was triggered by the Low Case falling below the Hedge Target. The new hedges were sized each time to remove just enough risk to lift the Low Case above the Hedge Target. Hedges were sized this way so that if the market recovered, the firm would have avoided placing any more hedges than were necessary. As it turned out, prices did not recover but continued to decline. By consistently adding hedges whenever the Low Case fell below the Hedge Target, the firm was able to protect and ultimately achieve its Hedge Target of $75/bbl., even though prices fell from above ninety dollars to below fifty dollars. To achieve this, as shown by the blue shaded area, the firm eventually had to hedge 95 percent of its production.

EXAMPLE: HEDGE TARGET OF $75MM FOR 2015

Initial hedges to a $75/bbl target reduced risk by 50%, but monitoring the "Hedge Target" alerted management on four occasions that additional hedges were needed to ensure budgetary success as prices fell.

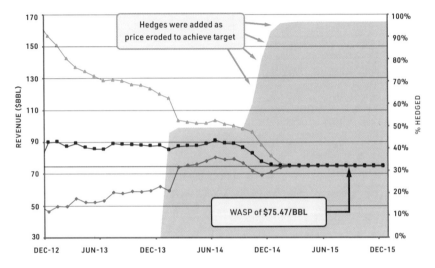

In weak markets, R^2 analytics alert management when additional

FIGURE 6-5

What would have happened if the company decided that being 50 percent hedged was their metric of success and just stayed there?

EXAMPLE: FIXED HEDGE PERCENTAGE FOR 2015

In 2015, a $48.80 settlement price yielded WASP of $68.43. Sharply lower prices resulted in a WASP well below the **$75.25 implied Hedge Target**. Note that the Low Case fell below target while prices were above $80/bbl.

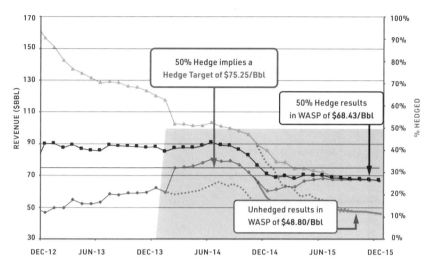

Fixed hedged volumes proved to be inadequate to achieve implied target.

FIGURE 6-6

Using a percentage hedged as their goal, this company would have stayed 50 percent hedged and would not have added hedges as prices started to erode. Using percentage hedged as the metric, they would not track or know that their Low Case would fall well below seventy-five dollars, as seen in figure 6-6. They achieved their goal of 50 percent hedged and management would likely remain confident they would be "successful" until it was too late to repair the damage. These hedges reduced risk and, in this case, helped the firm financially. But that may not have been enough. Using a percentage hedged as the target, management does not know how much risk it had, or has. It does not help management to plan for the future, respond to changing market conditions, or manage the financial health of their business. Many companies fail to respond to adversity in time or at all, and they face financial shortfalls or the risk of bankruptcy simply because they failed to use the right metric to manage risk.

PRM quantifies risk, enables management to identify a Hedge Target aligned with its business goals, and alerts them to take action when conditions deteriorate. PRM will give you time to react and to add more hedges, thereby guaranteeing a successful outcome. Hedging to maintain a minimum confidence level for a key success metric ensures that your business will achieve success in nearly all market conditions.

> Hedging to maintain a minimum confidence level for a key success metric ensures that your business will achieve success in nearly all market conditions.

A SERIES OF DECISIONS

PRM is a process of monitoring and responding to risk. Note that in the adverse price example, the successful firm met its target by evaluating risk each month and making several decisions to add hedges. Those new hedges were critical to their success. Like a baseball player who gets several swings at the plate, managing risk as a series of focused and measured decisions allows management to identify and defend a minimum performance target. If you confront a business with a large binary decision—hedge everything or nothing—chances are management would choose to do nothing. And if they act, it would be their one shot to get it right.

To use another sports analogy, football teams get four downs to succeed. It's what they do in each down, and the result of each play, that influences what they will do on the next down. If the quarterback gets sacked on the first down, both the offensive and defensive teams will use that information to develop their strategies for the next down. Or if a team has first and goal at the eight-yard line, their first-down play will look vastly different compared to if they were sixty yards downfield. They don't simply assume that because the outcome of the plays is unpredictable, perhaps random, they should stick with one strategy and use it all the time.

Now let's look at the larger picture. Typically, each offense in football gets the ball about six or seven series per half. That means each team gets twelve or thirteen opportunities to be on offense or "touch the ball" in each game and have an opportunity to advance or score. Contrary to what all the Monday-morning armchair quarterbacks have to say, there isn't a single play, fumble, catch, tackle, or penalty that is responsible for the total outcome of a game. Instead, it's a series of events where a decision is made and produces an outcome, and the result provides information used to make the next decision. Even though many fans look at the game plan in the final two minutes and complain that was where things went wrong, their team wouldn't have been in that position if they had been making more successful plays throughout the game.

The same applies to hedging with PRM. It is better to add hedges as needed, in small steps. If a firm ignored warnings and didn't hedge in the first two quarters, it might suddenly find itself faced with a decision to hedge 60 percent all at once. If the firm let itself get to this point, it's unlikely that they will do anything now. It's simply too large a decision to make, with too much riding on the outcome. The reason the firm got into this position is that, at least by default, it chose not to be hedged. To hedge a large amount now would mean the firm changed its strategy, essentially admitting it was wrong and wanting to have a *new* strategy. How does an individual or management team justify a change like that? Unfortunately, now that the firm is threatened, they should ask themselves what will happen if the firm hedges less than it should, or maybe even nothing at all. Unless the firm is lucky, it'll find that its troubles will worsen.

It is critical for companies to have a process in place to manage risk and to be disciplined throughout the whole process. This begins with developing and monitoring the metrics that define their success and allow them to quantify their risk exposure.

A SHIFT IN PERSPECTIVE

On occasion, it becomes necessary to shift the perspective on which metrics define success for a client in order to help them achieve their longer term strategic goals.

For instance, a utility came to us with a desire to hedge their fuel, which generated their electricity. We were hired to write a hedge policy document. But before we could do that, we needed to know what determined their success. Why were they hedging? They had three parties they ultimately needed to answer to: (1) shareholders, who wanted to be assured that their dividends would be paid; (2) ratepayers, who could not afford large increases in electricity rates; and (3) the government/public utility commission, who wanted to make sure that excessive costs were not being placed on ratepayers. By understanding this dynamic, we wrote language to address the needs of all three stakeholders. We incorporated these factors in the model we developed for them to identify the High Case–risked scenario for what the maximum tariff and minimum acceptable dividend would be. With that, we calculated the price of the maximum acceptable fuel cost and how much risk needed to be hedged away. Now the utility could monitor its risk as it related to the metric of success they were being evaluated by, explain to stakeholders why they were hedging, and hedge appropriately to defend the metric.

Success for this client had everything to do with the metrics that they needed to achieve for their stakeholders. Hedging the fuel was an important, but single, tool that would be used to achieve the desired result. Other tools might include modifying the shareholder dividend, investing in more efficient generation, or building a reserve to temporarily absorb higher fuel costs whenever prices surged. Note that, like hedging, each alternative is a finite resource. Each has its associated cost, whether it be to shareholders through a lower dividend, the utility by saddling it with additional debt obligations, or ratepayers through additional costs to fund a reserve. It is management's responsibility to evaluate the cost/benefit of the resources at their disposal. When hedging is accomplished using PRM, management and stakeholders are working together toward the same success metric.

> When hedging is accomplished using PRM, management and stakeholders are working together toward the same success metric.

R^2 ANALYTICAL TOOLS QUANTIFY RISK IN BUDGETARY TERMS AND ARE USED BY MANAGEMENT TEAMS TO IDENTIFY WHEN TO DO THE FOLLOWING:

- access more capital
- increase borrowing
- reduce expenditures
- hedge

> ## WHEN HEDGING IS APPROPRIATE, R^2 CLIENTS HEDGE:
>
> - to ensure budgetary goals are achieved
> - the volumes needed to do so
> - with the right instrument for them and the market conditions
> - in a time frame that allows them to achieve good pricing

To further illustrate, let's take the example of a new client who had to change their perspective. Shortly after oil prices fell by 25 percent, we got a phone call. Earlier in the year, this company was expecting $375 million in EBITDA. But then prices dropped significantly, and management hadn't responded; they had just watched as budgetary success slipped through their fingers. In a panic, they called us up and said, "How do we hedge to fix this?"

Unfortunately, the gate had been left open, and the horse had already run out of the barn. There was no sense in closing the gate now. That would only guarantee financial failure. First conversations like this are very painful. The new client still wanted to believe that a $375 million EBITDA was achievable, but they were now facing a $75 million shortfall. Unless they changed their earlier expectations, all they now had was hope that prices would recover.

But they did change, and all was not lost. By reframing their goals to investors and coming up with a new strategy, one that hedged everything to defend the current price and expanded their revolving credit to make up the expected shortfall, they were able to right the ship and lived to sail another day. Time can be a valuable tool—allowing management to push back its performance goal by one year or more—especially in instances when it provides a company the opportunity to save itself.

We want to emphasize that moving a performance target because of changing commodity prices should not be necessary. PRM will allow you to defend your target and avoid financial peril. The key to achieving success using PRM is identifying appropriate success metrics(s) and managing your risk proactively. If you defend your target(s), you'll achieve it. If you don't defend it ... good luck—you're at the mercy of the market.

And now that you know what to measure and manage to achieve success, we have to discuss which instruments to use and how to get them in place.

—————— **Chapter Assets** ——————

- PRM optimizes for success, which minimizes or eliminates failure.
- The "process" in PRM creates the opportunity to face a series of small decisions.
- Hedging is just one of several tools to manage risk.

CHAPTER SEVEN

Tactical Hedging

You've got to know when to hold 'em

Know when to fold 'em

Know when to walk away

And know when to run!

—**Kenny Rogers, "The Gambler"**

PRM ANALYTICS EMPOWER clients to proactively identify the strategic hedges they need (Risk Driven) and hedges they want (Market Driven). Once the decision has been made to place a strategic hedge and management has agreed upon how much risk should be removed, the next steps are tactical. From that perspective, the key questions are the following: Which hedge instrument are you going to use, and how aggressive are you going to be about getting those hedges in place?

HEDGE INSTRUMENTS—SIMPLIFIED

To begin this discussion, we ask you to consider that there are essentially just two hedge instruments: call and put options. Options are rights that are bought by one party and sold by another. The buyer pays for the right. The seller is paid for taking on the obligation. The careful selection of calls and puts, often in some combination of rights purchased and sold, will result in a hedge strategy with a payout profile that matches the hedger's specific needs. First, let's review what call and put options are.

Call options give the owner the right, but not the obligation, to buy a specific amount of the underlying commodity at a specific price (the option's strike price) for a limited period of time (until the expiration date). The option seller is paid a premium for agreeing to deliver the commodity (or its financial equivalent) under the contract terms. Call options with strike prices below the current market price are "in the money." If the strike price is near or equal to the market price, the options are considered "at the money," and if it is above the market price, they're "out of the money." Puts, on the other hand, give the buyer the right, but not the obligation, to sell the underlying commodity at a specific price for a limited period of time. Conversely, put options with strike prices above the current market price are "in the money." If the strike price is near or equal to the market price, puts are "at the money" and below the market price "out of the money."

Sometimes, hedgers will simply buy a call or put. Owning a call will protect a consumer from prices above the option's strike price and, because this is a right and *not* an obligation, allow them to benefit from lower prices. Of course, there is no free lunch. The owner would have to buy this option for the price at which it is trading, or its "premium," which is usually demanded upon purchase. That cost has an immediate impact on cash flow. For that reason and others, hedgers do not routinely purchase options as a strategy. *Routinely* does not mean "never." We will discuss the conditions when buying options should be considered later in this chapter.

Consider this from the option seller's point of view. The seller of the option collects a premium, but the obligation may result in a disproportionately larger loss. For this reason, most option sellers are "covered." That is, if the seller of an option must pay the buyer, they have other assets that will generate a proportional benefit at the same time. Some option sellers are professional traders, whose knowledge of and low-cost access to the markets enables them to manage this lopsided risk. Others are hedgers, willing to sell options because this lopsided risk is right-way risk. For example, if an oil producer sold calls and the price of oil went above the strike price of the calls, the producer would be obligated to pay the owner of the calls. As an asset owner, this cost would be offset by the higher-than-expected price they received for their production.

It is important to note that the cash received for the sold option would be of little commercial value to this producer. This is true, especially given the risk. For that reason, the selling of an option to collect cash is not considered a very good hedge, because most of the risk is not offset. However, selling options can make sense as part of a larger strategy. When the premium from sold options is used to purchase other options, which will themselves have a lopsided payout, the combination can result in an effective hedge strategy.

Let's begin with the most common hedge strategy: a swap. A swap can be thought of as a combination of an "at the money" call and an "at the money" put that have the same strike price, where one option is bought and the other sold to offset the premiums. Consumers, for example, would hedge by "buying" the swap, which means they buy an "at the money" call and sell an "at the money" put. To illustrate how this would lock in the price, let's assume the strike of these options is $50/bbl. If at expiration the market is above fifty dollars, the consumer will exercise the call owned to monetize the value between the option strike and the higher market price. The put would be worthless because the put owner would rather sell at the market price, which is higher than the strike price. When the market is below $50/bbl. at expiration, the consumer will be obligated to pay the owner of the put option, who would exercise their right to sell at fifty dollars. Who might the owner of the put be? It is likely that the owner would be a producer, who also desired a hedge and locked in the price of $50/bbl. In this example, the consumer gave away the right to benefit from lower pricing to assure it would pay $50/bbl. The producer gave away the right to benefit from higher prices to know it would receive $50/bbl. for their production.

> **LONG SWAP = LONG CALL + SHORT PUT,**
> where the strike prices are the same
>
> **SHORT SWAP = SHORT CALL + LONG PUT,**
> where the strike prices are the same

The next-most-popular hedge strategy, a collar, is a simple variant of the swap. It is an almost identical structure, except that there is a gap between the option strike prices. Normally, both options are "out of the money," which results in a higher strike price for the call than the put. Our consumer might have bought the call with a $55/bbl. strike price and sold a put with a $45/bbl. strike price. Now, both parties accept the risk that the price can float anywhere between forty-five dollars and fifty-five dollars. Neither has protection unless the commodity price exceeds one of the strike prices. The consumer will be paid if prices rally above fifty-five dollars, and only to the extent that prices are above fifty-five dollars. The producer will be paid if prices fall below forty-five dollars, and only to the extent that prices are below forty-five dollars. Again, the owner of the option receives payment when it is exercised, and the granter of the option is the one who pays.

LONG COLLAR = LONG CALL + SHORT PUT,
where the strike prices are different

SHORT COLLAR = SHORT CALL + LONG PUT,
where the strike prices are different

There are an endless number of strike price combinations and other (more complicated) structures that can be created by combining call and put options, such as participation swaps, three-ways, enhanced swaps, extendible options, double ups, and swaptions. The interested reader can look these up on the internet. As a rule, we advise clients to keep their instrument selection as simple as possible (swaps and collars). Simple hedge strategies ensure transparency on pricing, have lower embedded costs, and are easier to explain to stakeholders (including board members, large shareholders, and private equity investors). Experience has convinced us that complex hedge structures rarely offer a meaningful improvement over simple strategies. Worse, they complicate the decision process and distract management from the most important tactical issue—getting the hedge they need or want.

HEDGE INSTRUMENT SELECTION

Is hedging with swaps or collars preferred? To answer this question, the first thing to consider is your risk tolerance. You must decide if it's more important to maximize the risk mitigation benefit of hedging by locking in the current price (swap) or if keeping some of the risk (collar) is preferred. Maximizing the hedge benefit with swaps means that you can hedge less volume, but the price of your hedge is fixed, making your timing more important. Hedging with collars lets the price float between the strike prices and reduces the importance of timing. However, collars won't provide protection until the long option strike price is exceeded. Clearly, if collars are the desired hedge instrument, then serious consideration must also be given to the gap between strikes. Too wide and you won't get the hedge protection you need. Too narrow and you might as well have used a swap. Your first consideration must always be to select the hedge instrument that will efficiently mitigate the risk you can't afford to keep.

Common Strategies Compared

To continue this discussion of instrument choice, let's analyze the amount of risk mitigation between swaps and collars. Let's compare a long fifty-dollar swap that mitigates risk from $50/bbl. on up and a forty-five-dollar to fifty-five-dollar consumer collar that mitigates risk from $55/bbl. on up. If we assume that there is risk up to $70/bbl., the swap will provide $20/bbl. of risk mitigation (from $50/bbl. to $70/bbl.), while the collar will provide $15/bbl. of risk mitigation (from $55/bbl. to $70/bbl.). Hence, the swap offers 133 percent of the risk mitigation as the costless collar in this example.

If the consumer's enterprise had a risk of $20 million from rising oil prices and $18 million of risk was acceptable to make budget, it would need to reduce risk by $2 million. It could accomplish this with either of these hedge strategies:

- $2 million/($20/bbl. risk reduction) of swaps ➜ 100,000 bbl. of fifty-dollar swaps

OR

- $2 million/($15/bbl. risk reduction) of collars ➜ 133,000 bbl. of forty-five-dollar to fifty-five-dollar collars

We can see that, as measured by hedge instrument "effectiveness," swaps lead the way in risk reduction. They begin reducing risk immediately from the current price and require less volume to do the same mitigation. Collars do not protect until the long strike is exceeded. As this example demonstrates, the consumer is exposed not just to five dollars more of risk; it is the first and most probable five dollars of risk. Said another way, the option won't help until the consumer has already given up five dollars.

Sometimes the choice between instruments is driven completely by risk tolerance. Other times it is not a clear choice. When it is not, use market data to guide your decision.

LET THE MARKET HELP YOU

Commodity prices move in response to capital flowing into and out of the market. The direction of money moved and the rate at which it moves impacts price. The market's response to capital flow is registered as price movement, which gives clues to three important drivers responsible for short- and medium-term price direction: (1) in which direction the market is trending; (2) if the price of the market is relatively attractive; and (3) who is in control of the market. While these drivers are our secondary considerations after risk tolerance, they are especially useful (1) when the choice is not clear between whether to hedge with a swap or collar, and (2) with the timing of the hedge transaction by providing guidance on whether to go to the market now or to use a limit order, waiting for the market to come to you. Further, when collars are chosen, price data can help you determine how wide the gap should be between strike prices. The three drivers of the market provide information that is so important that we borrowed an acronym to help readers remember them: TLC—trend, location, and control.

Trend

Trend describes the current persistence of price to move directionally (i.e., up or down). Companies looking to hedge should always consider the current trend to decide how they need to respond to the market. There are many ways to measure trend, with moving averages perhaps being the most popular. A simple moving average will observe the average of the most recent n days and then update that number each day by dropping the oldest and including the newest close in the new average. Most analysts assume that when the new average is higher than the previous average, the trend is up. Lower, and they will assume the trend is down. Others might also require that for an uptrend, the aforementioned condition must be met and the current price must be above the average. Only then would they consider the trend to be up. It is beyond the scope of this book to offer you a preferred trend indicator, and there is no single best trend indicator. You will have to research trend indicators and decide which is best for your needs.

A key fact to know about trend indicators is that with a large enough data set (and one that begins and ends at the same price to avoid bias), selling when the trend turns down and buying when it turns up is a break-even game, at best. You can take our word for it or test for yourself across many different moving average calculations and calculation periods. Buying and selling trend changes may be profitable for short periods of time, but it can't be in the long run. If this wasn't the case, someone would be getting rich trading that algorithm. Fortunately, this fact should not disturb you. Why? You are not trying to profit from the market's movements but rather get a better-than-average price for your hedge. You are not going to be in the market long or often enough for you to need to guess how to buy low and sell high or sell high and buy low. You want to identify trend for the simple purpose of helping you decide if prices are more likely to help or hurt you while trying to place the hedge. Some of the most critical decisions you will have to make will be when the market is trending against you and it persists over an extended period. If you respect the trend, your decisions to hedge will protect your business.

> If you respect the trend, your decisions to hedge will protect your business.

Location

Location is an indicator of the relative attractiveness of price given its recent price history. Even though prices move around significantly, hedging behavior should be measured. To emphasize a point made earlier, whether you're a producer or a consumer, you should not exhibit the same behavior at $60/bbl. as you do at $90/bbl. Why would you? Location helps you to maintain perspective, cognizant of whether prices are relatively low or relatively high and how the current price impacts you, consumer or producer. Remember that markets are mean reverting. That means they will not stay at their lows or highs for very long and will seek to return to their average. Just look at any long-term commodity chart to convince yourself.

To identify location, take a statistical estimate of the range

(Bollinger Bands will do) and divide it into thirds; the lowest third is considered the Buy Zone, the highest third is the Sell Zone, and the middle third is the Neutral Zone. If you are hedging with collars, we suggest using the transition points between zones to identify price levels for option strike prices. Depending upon the market price, you may want the long option to provide protection before you enter the adjacent zone or prefer that the short option give you room to participate to an adjacent zone. The following decision matrices provide guidance on instrument choices using trend and location.

Consumer

TREND + LOCATION = INFLUENCES INSTRUMENT SELECTION

Trend + Location should influence the choice of hedge instrument.

	UP TREND	DOWN TREND
BUY ZONE	**SWAPS** take advantage of attractive location	**COLLARS** respect trend by retaining downside
SELL ZONE	**COLLARS** respect location by retaining downside	**CALLS** retain as much downside as possible

FIGURE 7-1

Producer
WHICH HEDGE INSTRUMENT IS PREFERRED?

Trend + Location should influence the choice of hedge instrument

	UP TREND	DOWN TREND
BUY ZONE	**PUTS** retain as much upside as possible	**COLLARS** respect location by retaining upside
SELL ZONE	**COLLARS** respect trend by retaining upside	**SWAPS** take advantage of attractive location

FIGURE 7-2

Since the decision matrix allows for the purchase of options, let's consider a third strategy: a simple call purchase. Long options can be an effective hedge strategy, but the market must be priced right. What if a consumer were to just purchase a fifty-five-dollar call alone for three dollars? Our risk mitigation would not begin until $58/bbl. (breakeven) and that three-dollar cost would be a constant, regardless of the commodity price, higher or lower. Inexperienced hedgers are often drawn to the simplicity of a call option. Be warned: over time, the purchase of options almost always proves to be an expensive proposition. On the one hand, an option purchase is like car insurance: you pay a premium to insure the vehicle against collision or theft, and the deductible (gap to the strike price) is the risk you take until the insurance kicks in and the insurer begins to pay you back for loss. Good enough. But the real cost is not just this year's premium. If you don't have an accident for several years, the true benefit of your car insurance is the money you received to repair your car less the sum of *all* premiums you have paid your insurer over the years.

Following this logic, one might expect that purchasing calls would only be advisable if the consumer was worried about a large, adverse move higher. But that would be incorrect. When higher prices are threatening, consumers should hedge with swaps at $50/bbl. instead of buying fifty-five-dollar calls. The swap will protect them on any move higher. After paying a three-dollar premium to buy fifty-five-dollar calls, the option hedge does not provide protection until $58/bbl. It may be counterintuitive, but the best time for a consumer to shell out a premium to buy a call option is when they believe the exact opposite—that lower prices are ahead.

Why would a consumer buy call options when they think prices are going down? The answer is that it is a great way to get risk reduction *and* benefit from lower prices. It is the reverse for producers. We had a producer client who was required to hedge (sell) in early 2009 after oil prices had just fallen from $147/bbl. to below $40/bbl. Who wants to lock in prices after they have fallen by more than $100/bbl.? We advised this client to buy puts with a $28/bbl. strike price for $1/bbl. and hope they go out worthless. The banks (who had extended loans) wanted protection and were happy that enough revenue was secured. In the months that followed, oil prices eventually recovered to $70/bbl. These puts provided the producer with the protection demanded by their lenders and allowed the client to ride prices back up to $70/bbl., a gain of more than $30/bbl. when compared to hedging with swaps. The client achieved this benefit because they were willing to forfeit $1/bbl. in premium and the prices were at a market extreme. If, at the same time, a consumer client had asked, hedging with swaps would have been our advice.

Control

Control identifies whether buyers are supporting prices and likely to push them higher or if sellers are pressuring them lower. Short-term trading behavior is driven by profitability. Observing the collective responses of all market participants identifies three key price thresholds: the prior week's high, low, and midpoint. The midpoint of the prior week's range is a good approximation for the Control Pivot. When prices are above the Control Pivot, buyers have the stronger hand. Conversely, with prices below the Control Pivot, sellers have the stronger hand. For example, let's say that last week prices ranged from $52/bbl. to $58/bbl. If the price is above the midpoint, fifty-five dollars, assume buyers have the stronger hand. Below fifty-five dollars, it is most likely that sellers are in control. When buyers push prices above last week's high or sellers below last week's low, that is further confirmation of their control. This gives us a simple but clear assessment of market strength and guidance on how to time our approach to the market.

Consumer

TREND + CONTROL = INFLUENCES HEDGE TIMING

Trend + Control should influence timing and/or the choice of "Market" vs. "Limit" orders.

	UP TREND	DOWN TREND
BUYERS IN CONTROL	**NO TIME TO WAIT** lift offers regardless of zone	**SOME FLEXIBILITY** use limit orders priced in neutral and sell zones
SELLERS IN CONTROL	**SOME FLEXIBILITY** use limit orders priced in neutral and sell zones	**TIME TO WAIT** use limit orders priced in buy zone

FIGURE 7-3

Producer

WHICH ORDER TYPE IS MOST APPROPRIATE?

Trend + Control should influence timing and/or the choice of
"Market" vs. "Limit" orders.

	UP TREND	DOWN TREND
BUYERS IN CONTROL	TIME TO WAIT use limit orders priced in sell zone	SOME FLEXIBILITY use limit orders priced in neutral and buy zones
SELLERS IN CONTROL	SOME FLEXIBILITY use limit orders priced in neutral and buy zones	NO TIME TO WAIT hits bid regardless of zone

FIGURE 7-4

TLC GUIDELINES ON MARKET STRENGTH

- PRM is a strategic tool that will identify when you should respond to market changes.

- Risk Driven hedge strategies are needed when risk exceeds your tolerance.

- Market Driven strategies take advantage of attractive pricing.

- Once hedging is desired, TLC will assist with the selection of a hedge instrument and the timing of the hedge.

- Respect the Trend.

- Trend and Location should influence hedge instrument selection.

- Trend and Control should influence hedge timing.

- Do not micromanage hedge decisions and lose sight of the big picture—risk mitigation.

- Don't fight yesterday's battle. Markets change constantly, and you must change with them. Be objective and goal oriented at all times.

All else being equal, we can build a table for how each instrument tactically benefits the hedger.

	RISK MITIGATION	PRICE PARTICIPATION
SWAP	1	3
COLLAR	2	2
LONG CALL/PUT	3	1
	1 = Best, 3 = Weakest	

Once the strategic decision to hedge has been made and you know how much risk needs to be reduced, the next steps are tactical. Use TLC (trend, location, and control) to assist with the choice of hedge instrument, calculate the needed hedge volumes, and determine how much time is available for you to hedge. In the following chapters, we take the process one step further, iterating the steps in a feedback loop to continually manage the amount of risk required amid changing market and enterprise conditions.

Chapter Assets

- There are just two hedge instruments, calls and puts, which can be bought or sold in a wide variety of combinations to achieve various payout profiles.
- Mitigate risk first, then optimize for conditions.
- Trend + Location = Strategy selection
- Trend + Control = Timing

Consumer Hedging

Grant me the strength to accept the things I cannot change, the courage to change the things I can, and the wisdom to know the difference.

—Reinhold Niebuhr

CONSUMER HEDGING is usually driven by budgetary goals. Typically, these are expressed in dollars per unit volume or in budgeted dollars (= $/unit × units) for a specific purpose. The overarching aim is to ensure that budgetary targets are achieved through a wide range of possible outcomes. In other words, consumers look to optimize, rather than maximize, performance.

We hope you now appreciate that to successfully manage budgetary performance, you cannot manage the price, but you *can* manage its risked price. If you like the price and it changes,

> Consumers look to optimize, rather than maximize, performance.

too bad—it's gone, because the market is trading at a new price. It might come back, but *if* and *when* are big uncertainties to hang your budget on. Remember, "hope is not an acceptable hedge strategy." If, however, a consumer wants to lower their High Case to reduce risk, that can be accomplished whether prices have moved lower *or* higher. The volume needed to achieve the reduction must be adjusted to compensate for current price, of course, but a hedge can be implemented that will still remove the desired amount of risk.

Since consumers are generally hedging costs that represent a component of overall expenses, it is important to keep those costs manageable so that the firm can focus its efforts on something it does have control of: its core competencies. Assuming a farmer is a buyer of diesel and propane, which represents 10 percent of annual costs, it will not matter if the cost fluctuates to 9 percent or 11 percent of the budget. But if the commodity moves up 50 percent, generating a 15 percent cost, that 5 percent additional cost could be a hit to the budget that removes most or all of the profit margin. Monitoring and managing expectations with a process ensures budgetary success by securing costs. This will enable the consumer to deliver budgetary success no matter where prices end up.

PRACTICAL APPLICATION OF RISK MANAGEMENT FOR COST CONTROL AND BUDGETING

- Express risk metrics in terms meaningful to decision makers.
- Understand that risk is a finite resource.
- Define revenues and/or profit margins in the context of risk and performance.
- Identify ranges of outcomes expressed in budgetary terms.

While a value at risk (VaR) measure is an effective way

to control and measure the performance of a trading group, it is an almost meaningless metric for capital-intensive activities like manufacturing. Traders are measured on their profitability, manufacturers on whether they achieved budget. An effective way to build a risk-based approach is to understand budgetary requirements and quantify the risks using key metrics that may impact performance. Once these risks are considered, a budget item can be expressed in terms of an expected amount and a budget-at-risk amount.

A SERIES OF DECISIONS

While the future is unpredictable, it can be simplified. Earlier in this book, we introduced the concept that from a hedger's perspective, a market can follow just four paths, expressed graphically as follows:

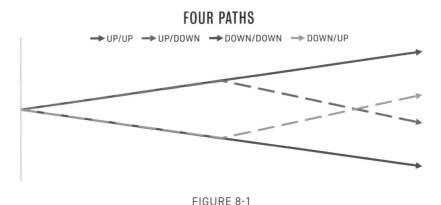

FOUR PATHS

→ UP/UP   → UP/DOWN   → DOWN/DOWN   → DOWN/UP

FIGURE 8-1

Now it is time to explore this in even more detail. In Chapter 5 we noted that market prices follow a serpentine and unpredictable path.

Figures 8-2 through 8-5 show some real-world market examples. The black line represents the market price, with the starting price to the far left. The orange line represents the average price observed during the hedge window, while the blue line represents the average prices in the settlement window or the average settlement price.

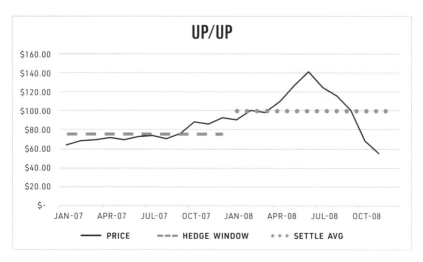

FIGURE 8-2

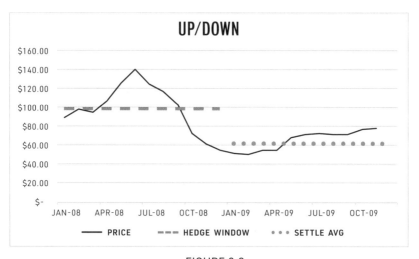

FIGURE 8-3

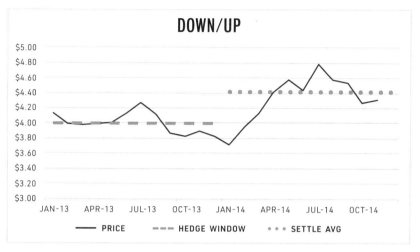

FIGURE 8-4

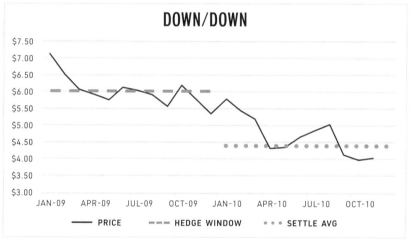

FIGURE 8-5

As evidenced in this example, the real world throws many curve balls at us. Prices don't move in a straight line but snake their way higher and lower, often producing the equivalent of head fakes that fool many people. This can result in their doing exactly the wrong thing at the most critical moments. This is where PRM's objective feedback loop shines by providing the data that management teams need to remain focused on the things they can and *should* manage.

141

PRM helps them to act proactively and keep their efforts proportionate to their needs through a series of informed decisions rather than a single all-or-none decision.

MARKET PATH: DOWN/DOWN

To return to a real-world example, let's look to natural gas. The first example we will examine has a down/down path. Here, the consumer never needs to add more hedges because prices moved lower throughout.

Consumer example 1: natural gas for Cal 2010

- Hedge window start price: $7.74

- Hedge window average price: $6.04 average during 2009

- Settlement window average price: $4.39 in 2010

- Market path: down/down

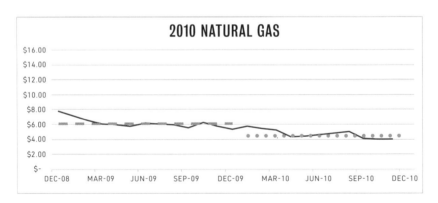

FIGURE 8-6

In figure 8-6, the start point (far left) is the highest price this swap achieved throughout this period (black line). Note that the swap's average price in the hedge window (orange line) is lower than the start price and then prices fell further in the settlement window (blue line).

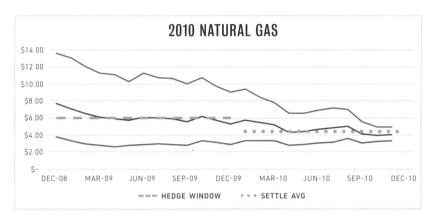

FIGURE 8-7

Throughout the hedge window, as shown in figure 8-7, both the High Case (red) and the Low Case (green) tracked the Base Case (black) closely. As time elapsed, these bands were consistently collapsing toward the Base Case. However, because during the hedge window there is still so much time before expiration that this factor is of secondary importance. Price and volatility are the drivers throughout the hedge window. Things change dramatically once we enter the settlement window. Now there is much less time remaining. Each month some portion of the hedge settles, which locks in a portion of the swap price and removes one-twelfth of the risk from the annual strip. During the settlement window, the risk bands collapse toward the Base Case rapidly.

As previously discussed, High Case and Low Case estimates are determined objectively from the implied volatility of option prices.

> High Case and Low Case estimates are determined objectively from the implied volatility of option prices.

HEDGING TO MANAGE THE HIGH CASE

Now we will demonstrate how to hedge in response to changes in the High Case. To do this, we will add a Hedge Target and then add hedges to pull the High Case below the Hedge Target whenever necessary. Each hedge will be in response to changes in the market.

Without hedges, the High Case for this swap was initially $13.60 (red line, far left), almost six dollars above the Base Case or swap price of $7.74 (black line). A consumer who is willing to pay $13.60 will budget their cost to a level. If in this example we set the Hedge Target to ten dollars (purple line, the maximum price for budgetary success), we see the High Case starts out above it. To pull the High Case down to the Hedge Target, we must remove about 60 percent of the risk, which will require a 60 percent hedge. As demonstrated in figure 8-8, the time hedges were added is shown with the blue shaded area (right axis). This pulled the High Case down to ten dollars (red line, left axis). Each month thereafter the swap price fell, which kept the High Case below the Hedge Target line. No additional hedges were ever needed to protect ten dollars.

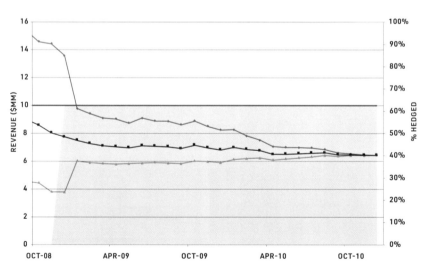

FIGURE 8-8

MARKET PATH: UP/UP

Now let's examine how the 2017 natural gas swap traded. Note below the key market features:

Consumer example 2: natural gas for Cal 2017

- Hedge window start price: $2.79

- Hedge window average price: $3.06 average during 2017

- Settlement window average price: $3.11 in 2017

- Market path: up/up

As you will see in the example shown in figures 8-9 and 8-10, the consumer added hedges whenever necessary, identified in those moments when the High Case rose above the Hedge Target. Each hedge was in response to changes in the market. If we just look at the observed prices between December 2015 and December 2017, we can see that this was a stable market that worked consistently higher. The Hedge Window average price was twenty-seven cents higher than the starting price, and the settlement average was five cents higher than the Hedge Window average.

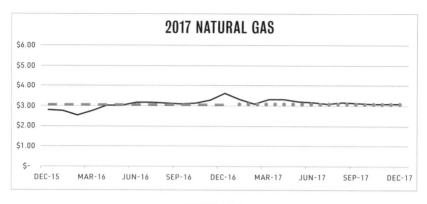

FIGURE 8-9

As we pointed out earlier, when we manage the risked price for consumers, that means the High Case (red).

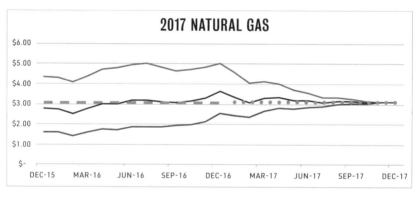

FIGURE 8-10

BUYING HIGH: TAKING THE EMOTION
OUT OF HEDGING DECISIONS

Hedging when prices rally can be very difficult for consumers. Most people want the lower price they saw previously and will be reluctant to pay today's higher price. Psychologists refer to this bias as *anchoring*. If someone tells you before you enter a car dealership that it will cost $20,000 to purchase the car you are targeting but then once you arrive you are told it will now cost $26,000, you are much less likely to buy the car because you were mentally anchored to the lower price.

Similarly, the constant stream of commodity prices can produce emotional confusion that, in hedging, can cause decision makers to behave like a deer in headlights. Rather than acting when they should, they make the mistake of waiting for the market to come back to some arbitrary price they've chosen as important. Then, to compound the problem, when they are lucky enough to get a second chance, often they back away from the opportunity and refuse to hedge because they begin to second-guess themselves. PRM takes the emotion out of hedging by providing objective information that allows you to control how much

> **PRM takes the emotion out of hedging and avoids price anchoring.**

risk you have (the thing you can control) and to stop thinking about price (the thing you can't control).

Let's take a simple example for a consumer of natural gas, W&A Electronics. W&A manufactures porcelain insulators, for which natural gas is used to heat the kilns to cure the clay. Their demand is very steady, and at current prices their profit margin is attractive. They've decided that hedging would improve their chances of a successful year, but they are not sure how much or when to hedge.

W&A decides that they will consider hedging for calendar year 2017 a year earlier, beginning December 31, 2015 (same data shown in the "up/up" example). At that time, gas swaps for 2017 are trading $2.79. The company likes that price but would rather not lock all of it in. Trying to estimate how much this price could change, they risk it statistically. The High Case estimate is $4.35, and the Low Case estimate is $1.63. If they had to pay $4.35 for the gas, it would not be a good year. Management decides that for this to be a successful year, their gas costs must be capped at $4.00/MMBtu. Their initial hedge is for 20 percent of their projected consumption at $2.79. Now, the weighted average hedge price, assuming they pay $4.35 on the remaining eighty percent of their fuel, is the $4.00 maximum they have targeted.

The next couple of months, prices drop. Throughout this period, their High Case stayed below the $4.00 target. Then in March, prices rallied high enough to push their High Case over $4.00. A small incremental hedge of 3 percent at $2.53 was enough to bring the High Case back to $4.00. But the next month, prices climbed to $3.01, which pushes the High Case to $4.27. New hedges are needed at $2.77 and are placed for an additional 16 percent of the volumes. That brings the High Case back down to $4.00. Now W&A has a total of 39 percent of the projected usage hedged.

Additional small hedges of 3 percent, 4 percent, and 2 percent are added in the following months, the last of which was placed at $3.18. The High Case remains below threshold right up until the end of 2016, when another 1 percent hedge is added at $3.29.

W&A made a series of six incremental hedges to keep the maximum targeted cost of four dollars (purple) at or below the High Case (red). In this example they hedged a total of 49 percent of their volumes at an average price of $2.93. Taking this example to completion, no additional hedges were required to maintain confidence that budget would be achieved. The averaged settled price was $3.11, and the weighted average cost of gas with hedges was $3.02.

If you hedge to maintain a target, you can reasonably expect to achieve the target.

If you hedge to maintain a target, you can reasonably expect to achieve the target.

The following series of graphs demonstrate how hedges were added as prices rose over time.

HEDGE IMPACT AS OF 11/30/2015

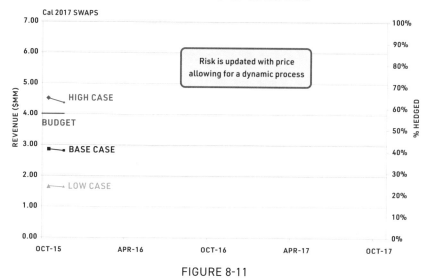

FIGURE 8-11

HEDGE IMPACT AS OF 3/31/2016

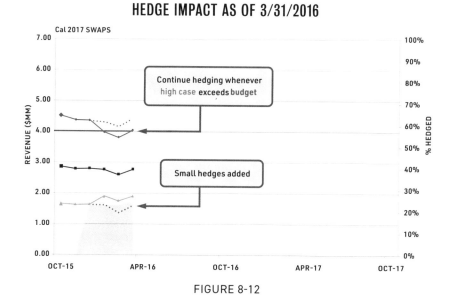

FIGURE 8-12

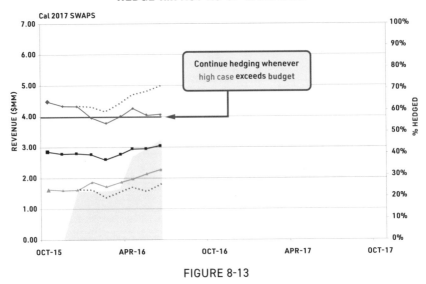

FIGURE 8-13

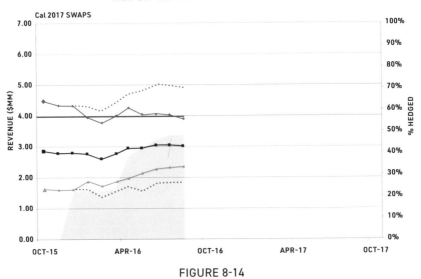

FIGURE 8-14

HEDGE IMPACT AS OF 12/31/2016

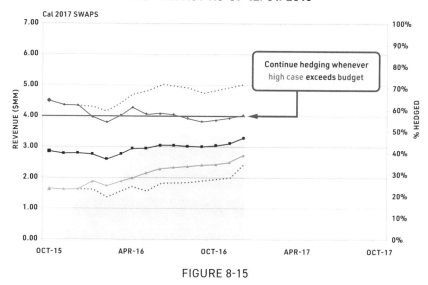

FIGURE 8-15

HEDGE IMPACT AS OF 3/31/2017

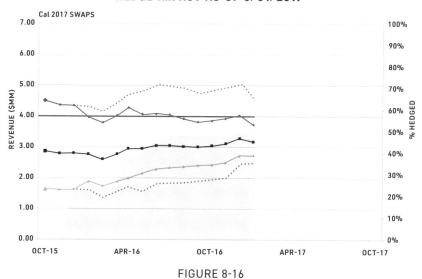

FIGURE 8-16

HEDGE IMPACT AS OF 6/31/2017

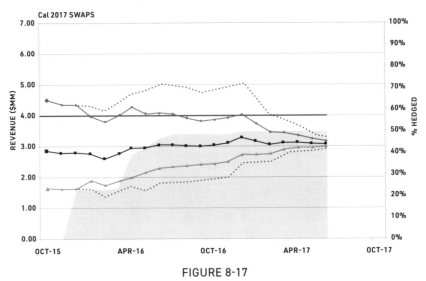

FIGURE 8-17

HEDGE IMPACT AS OF 10/31/2017

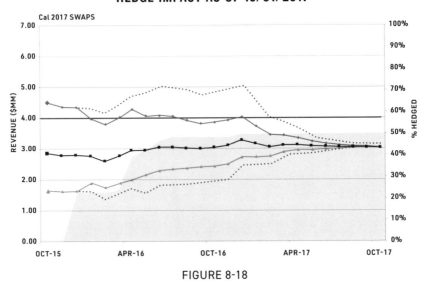

FIGURE 8-18

Proactive versus Reactive

In 2017, settlement prices ranged from a $2.63 low to a high of $3.93, averaging $3.11. W&A employed PRM to contain their risk. They hedged proactively whenever their High Case exceeded their Hedge Target. Following the guidance from PRM, they were never in jeopardy of paying more than $4.00 for gas. If they had not hedged, at one point the High Case would have exceeded five dollars when the market was trading $3.63. It is our experience that this is precisely the moment many holdouts will finally capitulate and hedge. Whether it is fear or fatigue, when the hedge is reactionary, it is usually at a terrible price. Why does this happen so often?

> Whether it is fear or fatigue, when the hedge is reactionary, it is usually at a terrible price.

Consider this: Mike Tyson, the former championship boxer, when asked about an opponent, said that "everyone has a plan until they get punched in the mouth." For those who manage commodity price risk, be warned that the market has an uncanny ability to "punch participants in the mouth." It is good at finding pressure points and squeezing participants until they are forced to make a decision. That's when things can get ugly. If management has waited too long, their decision will require a significantly larger response, one that is difficult to approve. If large enough, the pressure can then snowball throughout the firm because a large decision may require management approval. This, in turn, will require even more time to get key decision makers on board. While building consensus, if the price worsens, then an even larger hedge at a much higher price will be required. It is possible for the price to rally to or above four dollars before authorization is obtained. At four dollars, a 100 percent hedge would be required, but it would save the company! Above four dollars, the firm will miss budget and can only hope for another chance to hedge at lower prices.

When PRM is not employed, emotions can tie up the decision process, leaving management to hope for the best until they are faced with the worst. Then, when management reacts, they may find themselves doing the most harm at the worst possible price. In sharp contrast, PRM supports a proactive management of risk by breaking it down into smaller hedge decisions; in this example, six separate hedge decisions of 23 percent, 1 percent, 16 percent, 3 percent, 4 percent, and 2 percent were made.

In the final analysis, by employing PRM, the price W&A paid, inclusive of their hedges, was $3.02. This was not the low price they might have locked in when they started hedging, but it is well below budget and, in this case, below the market price of $3.11 for the settlement period in 2017.

CASE STUDY
University Protecting Budgetary Targets

CLIENT: Major university with multiple campuses.

PROBLEM: The university sets its budget during the fall, including its budget to heat the university's classrooms and dorms throughout the winter. The amount of fuel and funds needed to provide heat are unpredictable because they are largely driven by two unknowns: heating degree days (HDD) and energy prices.

CHARACTERIZATION: The university's fuel needs are seasonal and variable. R^2 analyzed the university's historical fuel usage, HDD, and fuel prices for the previous five years to identify baseload fuel usage levels, which could be managed separately from weather-driven demand usage.

SOLUTION: A strategy was approved to hedge baseload levels of fuel with physical forward fuel purchases and/or financial hedge instruments. It was implemented through a systematic process of hedging, with volumes added using a price/time approach. At each meeting, the hedge committee identified and approved a target hedge price. If the price was achieved before the next meeting, the hedge was placed. If it was not achieved, the hedge would be reviewed in the next hedge meeting.

RESULTS: The university was primarily interested in budget certainty, which led the hedge committee to complete hedging fuel for the next fiscal year before the budget was proposed. One driver was the observation that fuel costs were well below historic levels, enabling a Market Driven or opportunistic hedge decision, because baseload fuel costs were within budget. Locking in this price allowed the university to fund capital expenditures for maintenance, replacement, and upgrades to infrastructure. During times of budget tightening, additional certainty around fuel costs might have been used by the university to maintain staff and cut fewer services.

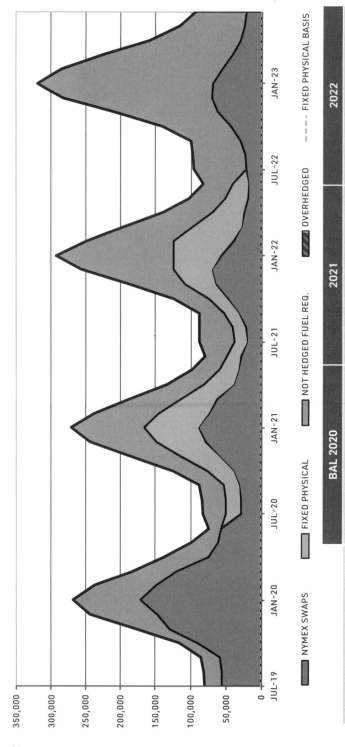

NATURAL GAS IN MMBTU/MONTH

FIGURE 8-19

EPILOGUE: The university chose to hedge their baseload demand usage because prices were attractive relative to those that they had paid in the recent past. Yet they remained mindful to keep hedged volumes to less than their expected full weather-driven fuel usage (as mandated by their hedge policy). The hedge committee was able to assure management that the university was not overhedged and had positioned itself to benefit if prices continued to work lower on those volumes that remained not hedged. Another key to the success of this program was the continuity of the hedge program. When hedges cost money at settlement, it was because natural gas prices continued to go lower, reducing cost to budget. The university's ongoing hedge efforts allowed them to benefit from these lower prices by adding new hedges.

CASE STUDY

Utility Protecting Capital Investment

CLIENT: Utility that upgraded generation units to enable fuel switching.

PROBLEM: A utility planned on spending $150 million to upgrade its electrical generation units to allow fuel switching. The units were originally built to burn fuel oil, the cheapest fuel at the time. However, in recent years natural gas and propane prices fell and generator efficiencies improved. The new economics meant that these fuels were less expensive and offered attractive savings to the utility and its ratepayers. If the utility could switch fuels to burn propane, at current prices they estimated they would save more than $30 million per year in fuel costs. Serving a population of just over 100,000 people, this was a great opportunity to save approximately $300 per person per year. The upgrade was expected to take eighteen months.

SOLUTION: The key to hedging this project properly was that once the capital was committed, the utility had passed the point of no return and was at risk. When the utility received the go-ahead for the project, R^2 began assisting the client to hedge propane in a three-year period beginning six months after the planned go-operational date. This six-month window allowed for the possibility of some construction delays. Hedges for the first year of the three-year hedge window were the priority, but all three years were hedged to lock in planned economics.

RESULTS: Construction delays were longer than allowed for, which required that hedges covering the first year be rolled to later years. Specifically, hedge buys in the first year were sold and replaced with buys in later years. In some cases (but not all), this was to the utility's advantage, because the price they sold was higher than the new purchase price. Periodic price weakness allowed the utility to opportunistically hedge by accelerating the addition of more hedge volumes whenever prices dipped. Despite construction delays and a period through which propane prices more than doubled, project economics were achieved, and ratepayers were the direct beneficiaries. The hedges were successful because they locked in favorable economics that saved the utility more than $37 million.

CONCLUSION: Project economics are at risk once capital is committed. In this case, given that propane prices rallied from a low of thirty-three cents to a high of ninety-eight cents per gallon, hedging was an important component of the utility's strategy to lower power costs.

DEFENSIVE HEDGES: WHICH HEDGE THRESHOLD IS BEST FOR CONSUMERS?

Which hedge threshold you choose should match your risk tolerance, because it will protect you against adverse prices and avoid budgetary failure in key years. However, the threshold you choose is not expected to impact your average price over a long period of time. This means that with PRM you'll take the risk of budgetary failure out of the equation and do so without expecting to pay a large premium for this insurance. There are insights to be gained from modeled results. To demonstrate, we have modeled the performance of defensive hedges by compiling twelve years of pro forma results.

For WTI we observed the weighted average cost (WAC) data for six different hedge programs. Half of these programs had a twenty-four-month Hedge Window and half had a twelve-month Hedge

Window. Both had a twelve-month Settlement Window. To illustrate how the Hedge Targets were determined for the following table, take, for example, a Hedge Window where the starting price of crude oil was $60, and the High Case was $120.

- No hedge = never hedged results in the swap settlement price

  □ Hedge Target = none

- 50 percent of target = the target is to maintain hedges to 50 percent of starting risk

  □ e.g., Hedge Target of $90 = (start price + start High Case)/2 = ($60 + $120)/2

- 75 percent of target = the target is to maintain hedges to 75 percent of starting risk

  □ e.g., Hedge Target of $105 = (50 percent target + start High Case)/2 = ($90 + $120)/2

- SR = the target is to maintain hedges to the start High Case

  □ e.g., Hedge Target of $120 = High Case

The table (Figure 8-20) provides the WAC of WTI oil by (1) year (no hedges); (2) for each of the three various Hedge Targets; and (3) for strategies that began twelve and twenty-four months prior to the settlement window. On the far right of the table shown is the average performance achieved over the twelve years and the price difference from the "no hedge" strategy or the average settlement price of WTI.

Despite using six different hedge threshold calculations, in each case the average price paid did not differ in a meaningful way from the average WTI price during this period. Note that in years when settled prices were higher than in the previous year, the "no hedge" program (top row) generally resulted in the highest-priced oil (highest price is shaded in green; lowest price is shaded in yellow). When prices were lower than in the previous year, one of the hedge programs could be expected to perform worst. Looking across all the consumer hedge programs in oil, on average they experienced a pro forma loss of about one dollar when compared to not hedging. On the surface, that may not seem attractive, but neither does paying for insurance until you need it. There are two points we'd like to make here:

- The most important benefit was that budget was achieved each year with certainty.

- Oil prices without hedges experienced year-on-year changes that averaged $16.30/bbl. The hedge programs reduce that significantly, ranging from a low of $11/bbl. for the 50 percent of risk to a high of about $14/bbl. for the starting risk. The lower your risk threshold, the more you will hedge and reduce volatility.

CONSUMER WTI

	WTI2007	WTI2008	WTI2009	WTI2010	WTI2011	WTI2012	WTI2013	WTI2014	WTI2015	WTI2016	WTI2017	WTI2018	AVG	DIFF
NO HEDGE	$72.34	$99.65	$61.80	$79.53	$95.12	$94.20	$97.97	$93.00	$48.80	$43.32	$50.95	$64.77	$75.12	$(0.95)
50% 12	$65.84	$82.45	$95.95	$71.31	$87.51	$91.46	$93.45	$92.57	$69.88	$53.28	$48.57	$60.64	$76.07	$(2.29)
75% 12	$69.09	$89.95	$99.80	$75.20	$91.31	$93.63	$95.70	$92.78	$60.80	$48.30	$49.60	$62.70	$77.41	$(3.62)
SR 12	$72.34	$97.45	$103.66	$79.09	$95.12	$95.80	$97.96	$93.00	$51.72	$43.32	$50.64	$64.74	$78.73	$0.81
50% 24	$64.98	$82.62	$62.76	$81.61	$77.68	$85.91	$91.72	$88.97	$70.35	$70.43	$59.55	$55.07	$74.30	$0.04
75% 24	$69.56	$89.97	$61.47	$78.96	$85.57	$90.29	$93.96	$91.52	$60.72	$64.10	$56.18	$58.67	$75.08	$(0.37)
SR 24	$72.34	$96.71	$59.91	$76.36	$92.34	$94.02	$96.52	$93.00	$51.99	$57.81	$52.81	$62.05	$75.49	

■ = highest average that year   ■ = lowest average that year

FIGURE 8-20

CONSUMER NG

	NG2007	NG2008	NG2009	NG2010	NG2011	NG2012	NG2013	NG2014	NG2015	NG2016	NG2017	NG2018	AVG	DIFF
NO HEDGE	$6.86	$9.03	$3.99	$4.39	$4.04	$2.79	$3.65	$4.41	$2.66	$2.46	$3.11	$3.09	$4.21	$(0.87)
50% 12	$8.08	$8.86	$8.04	$6.07	$5.23	$3.93	$4.01	$4.41	$3.30	$2.96	$2.94	$3.11	$5.08	$(0.60)
75% 12	$7.52	$8.95	$7.97	$5.23	$4.63	$3.38	$3.83	$4.34	$3.02	$2.71	$3.02	$3.10	$4.81	$(0.34)
SR 12	$6.95	$9.03	$7.91	$4.39	$4.04	$2.83	$3.65	$4.41	$2.74	$2.46	$3.09	$3.09	$4.55	$(0.83)
50% 24	$6.04	$8.70	$6.06	$6.64	$6.29	$4.91	$4.56	$4.64	$3.48	$3.49	$3.39	$2.96	$5.03	$(0.53)
75% 24	$6.32	$8.88	$5.07	$5.84	$5.52	$4.03	$4.17	$4.48	$3.10	$3.18	$3.23	$3.00	$4.73	$(0.17)
SR 24	$6.62	$9.01	$4.10	$5.05	$4.76	$3.15	$3.78	$4.32	$2.72	$2.86	$3.07	$3.04	$4.37	

■ = highest average that year   ■ = lowest average that year

FIGURE 8-21

Moving on to natural gas, it is important that we remind you that gas prices fell by two-thirds between 2007 and 2018, from nine dollars to three dollars. Consumer hedge programs are early buyers and consequently suffered hedge losses when prices fall. (We urge you to read in the next chapter how this worked to the benefit of natural gas producers.)

Because gas prices fell with remarkable consistency, not hedging resulted in the lowest-price gas in most years and on average. Simply put, the more you hedged, the more you paid for gas. Does this mean that the gas hedges were a failure? Absolutely not! A better metric of performance is the discount to budget that was paid by the consumer, where the average price paid is compared to the budget price. When the initial High Case was the target (SR), this avoided hedges initially and usually reduced hedged volumes. The price these strategies paid for natural gas averaged 47 percent below target. Compare that to when 50 percent of the risk was initially removed with hedges; with that target defended, prices still beat budget but paid on average a modest 31 percent below target.

Another important observation is that the discounts below the risked targets for consumers are greatest in down/down markets, when hedging is normally minimized, and smallest in up/up markets, when the largest volumes are typically hedged. Nonetheless, in every year, under all market conditions, and at each level of risk tolerance, budget certainty was achieved because the price paid was always under the Hedge Target.

You may be asking, "How did R^2's clients generate the gains they did if the pro forma analysis breaks even?" Simply, the pro forma results shown here do not allow for Market Driven hedges. For this period, oil consumers were expected to make budget and nearly break even. Gas consumers made budget but did not achieve gains through this period. In hindsight, the consistent down/down pattern of the gas market was an obstacle that was too great to overcome. However, all hedge programs should strive for every advantage on each hedge to reduce costs. We cannot predict what the market's pattern will be. The best we can do is to optimize our hedge timing with PRM and, when the opportunity presents itself, place Market Driven or opportunistic hedges.

If we consider R^2's client hedge performance in aggregate, the choices they made to add Market Driven hedges are largely responsible for the hedge gains they achieved. Our clients are the orchestrators of these decisions and deserve full credit. PRM played a key role by identifying exceptional opportunities for them, but they made the decisions. There are many factors that might support adding Market Driven hedges. Sometimes the margins are too attractive to pass up; other times the fundamentals and the price do not make sense. Some clients simply leave limit orders at attractive levels over a consistent time interval. If they are filled, great.

Search for advantages, even small ones, when placing hedges. As an example, by using the same period of the month or year, we have been able to assist a major airline and an institutional gas buyer to extract a small but measurable edge that resulted in improved performance when compared to a randomly timed hedge program. If the consumer is going to be hedging, and as long as that commitment will be consistent, it makes sense to time Market Driven hedge buying at statistically attractive and/or opportune moments. While past gains are not an indication of future results, our clients collectively have demonstrated that hedge gains are achievable.

Chapter Assets

- Consumers focus on budget.

- Hope is not an acceptable hedge strategy.

- Consumers must buy high when risk thresholds are challenged.

- When consumers are confronted with a down/down path, hedges will lose money, but they will beat budget.

- Lacking a budgetary target, consumers can instead defend the low-water mark of their High Case.

- Increased hedging results in reduced volatility but cannot be expected to impact the average cost over time.

- Market Driven hedges can improve hedge performance.

CHAPTER NINE

Producer Hedging

Luck is what happens when preparation meets opportunity.

—Seneca, Roman philosopher

PRODUCER HEDGE PROGRAMS and consumer hedge programs share many similarities. Both are best served when Hedge Targets are aligned with budgetary metrics and employ PRM as a feedback loop to monitor and maintain performance. Producer hedging, however, is the inverse of consumer hedging, and the Hedge Targets used span a much broader range of financial metrics.

Producer hedging protects against *lower* rather than *higher* prices. While higher prices negatively impact budgets for consumers, they are a producer's lifeblood. For producers, prices drive revenue, and revenue determines whether they are successful or fail. Everything begins with revenues, yet with the exception of start-ups, producers rarely use revenue as the metric for hedges. Usually, producers work closely with their lenders (banks), who tend to focus on financial metrics other than revenue to measure success.

MOTIVATIONS FOR COMMODITY PRODUCERS TO HEDGE

- Targeted financial metrics
- Securing dividend payment
- Making debt service payments
- Funding capital expenditures
- Mergers and acquisitions (M&A) growth initiatives
- Maintaining and/or increasing the redetermination of borrowing base (RBL)
- Reducing volatility of earnings for higher P/E multiple
- Locking in opportunistic conditions
- Hold leases by production

A commodity producer defines success as meeting minimum operational performance metrics that may include revenue, free cash flow (FCF), EBITDA, or internal rate of return (IRR). A producer's success is largely dependent on the underlying price of the commodity it drills, mines, or harvests. Hedging is a direct and efficient tool to guarantee minimum levels of income. And it is one of the most transparent and efficient forms of insurance commercially available anywhere.

Consumer hedge program success is generally defined by budget certainty. Producer hedge program success is generally defined by financial results.

INTO THE METRICS

In figure 9-1, you can see that this firm is tracking both revenue and EBITDA changes from last month to the current month. For them,

PERFORMANCE RISK DASHBOARD

Lower Oil and NG prices reduced revenue and EBITDA estimates this past month.

YEAR	BASE CASE	AUG 31 2019 ($ MM)	JUL 31 2019 ($ MM)	PERCENT CHANGE	W & A BASE CASE VERSUS COMMODITY PRICES (PERCENT CHANGES)		
2019	Revenues	487	492	(0.9%)	Revenues	487	(0.9%)
	EBITDA	233	237	(1.5%)	EBITDA	233	(1.5%)
					WTI	$56.24	(2.8%)
					NG	$2.59	0.0%
2020	Revenues	425	458	(7.2%)	Revenues	425	(7.2%)
	EBITDA	173	203	(15.0%)	EBITDA	173	(15.0%)
					WTI	$52.17	(7.4%)
					NG	$2.40	(3.5%)
2021	Revenues	466	497	(6.2%)	Revenues	466	(6.2%)
	EBITDA	205	233	(12.1%)	EBITDA	205	(12.1%)
					WTI	$50.39	(6.1%)
					NG	$2.45	(3.5%)

FIGURE 9-1

EBITDA is the real driver.

The horizontal bars are colored red, indicating the values are lower in the current month than they were the month before. If values had increased, the bars would have been colored green. Essentially, this producer is worse off now than they were a month ago. In fact, their baseline revenues fell by 7.2 percent for 2020 and 6.2 percent for 2021. The firm's EBITDA fell even more than their revenues, by 15.0 percent in 2020 and 12.1 percent in 2021.

If we move now to figure 9-2, we can see that the EBITDA data presented above is presented as box plots for each year: 2019, 2020, and 2021. A more detailed look at this information identifies the 90 percent confidence intervals (light-shaded range) and the 50 percent confidence interval (dark-shaded range) and compares their risked estimates to their EBITDA target (purple line). The purple line is the producer's Hedge Target, the EBITDA they need, while the black dot is the Base Case. In 2019, this firm is in good shape with their Low Case well above their Hedge Target.

Unfortunately for this firm, prices in 2020 and 2021 are too low for them to achieve the Hedge Target. Note that the target is above the Base Case (black dot) in each year. That means that if they did hedge now, they would lock in prices that would guarantee they would *not* achieve target. See "High Water Mark for the Low Case" later in this chapter for one solution to address this situation.

RISKED EBITDA ESTIMATES BY YEAR

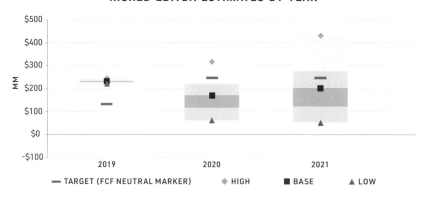

$ MM	2019			2020			2021		
	◆ HIGH	■ BASE	● LOW	◆ HIGH	■ BASE	● LOW	◆ HIGH	■ BASE	● LOW
EBITDA	247	233	224	319	173	63	435	205	54
Upside/Risk	14		(10)	146		(110)	230		(150)
Target (CAPX)		136			249			249	
EBITDA Minus Target (FCF)	112	98	88	70	(76)	(186)	186	(44)	(194)
WTI Price Deck (Full Year)	$59.92	$56.24	$53.16	$76.75	$52.17	$33.22	$81.54	$50.39	$28.24
NG Price Deck (Full Year)	$2.76	$2.59	$2.46	$3.50	$2.40	$1.56	$3.65	$2.45	$1.55

FIGURE 9-2

CASE STUDY

Client: Oil producer.

PROBLEM: A commodity producer was considering a $200 million acquisition. Because it was coming during a period when they were already expanding rapidly, they wanted to increase confidence that gross revenues and net cash flows would be adequate.

SOLUTION: The producer priced swaps for the next

five years to consider locking in much of the value of the proven reserves they'd own after this acquisition. They estimated that by hedging this production with swaps, they would lock in $60 million of crude oil sales (notional value) and remove $29 million in risk.

CONCLUSION: The client was confident that they could successfully take on the additional risk of this new asset if they hedged. Without hedging, they would have otherwise been risk averse and passed on the acquisition because of existing commitments. Hedging the proven reserves with swaps locked in 30 percent of the purchase price. This hedge was put in place as soon as they knew they would complete the transition, long before they owned the new acquisition. Hedging was the springboard that allowed this firm to maintain cash flow at levels they needed from proven reserves to fund the expenditures that would improve the undeveloped acreage in the new asset. With the hedge, this company increased their value through the acquisition and accelerated their growth by improving the new asset.

So what does a healthy company look like? Let's take a moment and walk through each step of the financial analysis in figures 9-3 through 9-9. First, we begin by risking prices to identify risked price estimates for our confidence intervals for each commodity in each budgetary period.

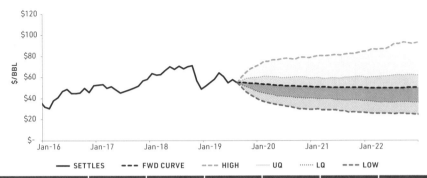

WTI HISTORICAL SETTLES AND FWD CURVE WITH RISK BANDS

WTI	2018	2019 YTD	AUG 2019	BAL 2019	2020	2021
High				$65.64	$76.75	$81.54
Upper Quartile (UQ)				$58.81	$60.22	$59.67
Settles/Fwd Curve	$64.77	$57.07	$54.84	$54.58	$52.17	$50.39
Lower Quartile (LQ)				$50.29	$42.31	$38.88
Low				$45.35	$33.22	$28.24

FIGURE 9-3

Risking one commodity would look like the above graph. But as we discussed in chapter 5, we use Monte Carlo simulations to collectively risk each of the commodities that constitute the firm's assets. This allows us to account for the noncorrelation effect between asset classes, accurately simulate their collective performance to create a sampling of possible revenue paths, and organize these paths into a risked distribution of possible revenue generation. With that, we can use base and risked revenue estimates to develop High-, Base-, and Low-Case performance estimates initially for revenues, which are then modified into other key financial metrics.

ANALYTICS APPLIED TO YOUR BOTTOM LINE

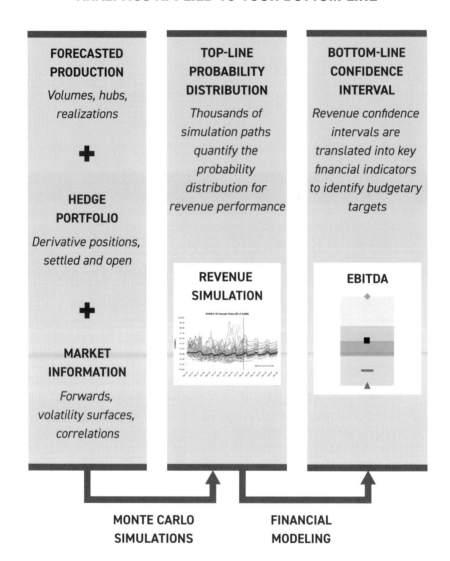

FORECASTED PRODUCTION

Volumes, hubs, realizations

+

HEDGE PORTFOLIO

Derivative positions, settled and open

+

MARKET INFORMATION

Forwards, volatility surfaces, correlations

TOP-LINE PROBABILITY DISTRIBUTION

Thousands of simulation paths quantify the probability distribution for revenue performance

REVENUE SIMULATION

BOTTOM-LINE CONFIDENCE INTERVAL

Revenue confidence intervals are translated into key financial indicators to identify budgetary targets

EBITDA

MONTE CARLO SIMULATIONS   **FINANCIAL MODELING**

R^2'S DETAILED RISK MODELING PROVIDES CLIENTS WITH A UNIQUE VIEW OF THEIR RISK

FIGURE 9-4

As shown in Figure 9-5, this firm has $150 million of risk (Base Case of $300 million – Low Case $150 million = $150 million of risk).

CONFIDENCE INTERVAL

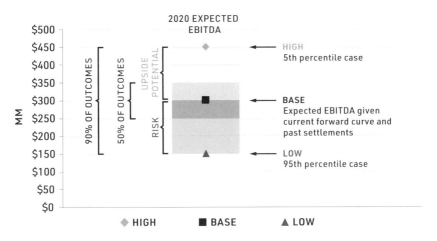

R^2 clients are provided objective confidence intervals for their bottom-line performance based on current forward curves and volatility surfaces.

FIGURE 9-5

The shown Hedge Target of $200 million EBITDA (Fig. 9-6) is needed to cover dividends, interest, and CAPX, indicating the firm has $50 million more risk than is acceptable.

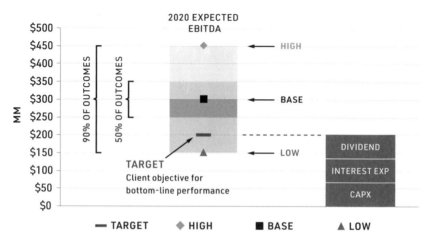

Management targets are assessed in relation to these confidence intervals.
Quantified hedge decisions are taken to achieve desired levels of risk.

FIGURE 9-6

By hedging enough to eliminate $50 million of risk (Fig. 9-7),
the Low Case is raised to their Hedge Target of $200 million. This
lowers the High Case, which fell from $450 million to $400 million.

POST HEDGE

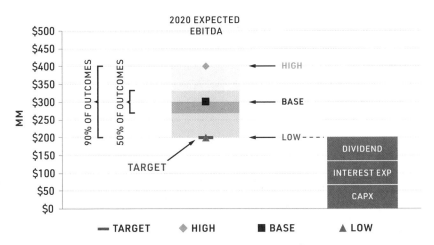

Hedge decisions manage both upside potential and downside risk. Risk is monitored so targets can be protected as prices change.

FIGURE 9-7

To illustrate analytics for the current and next two years, Figures 9-8 and 9-9 provide results from a different company. In each year the Low Case is above the Hedge Target, indicating that risk is within tolerance and additional hedges are not required at this time.

RISKED EBITDA ESTIMATES BY YEAR

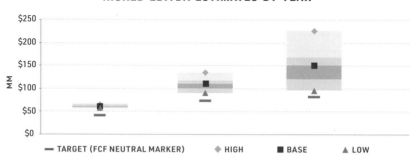

$ MM	2019			2020			2021		
	◆ HIGH	■ BASE	● LOW	◆ HIGH	■ BASE	● LOW	◆ HIGH	■ BASE	● LOW
EBITDA	61	58	55	137	110	88	221	149	98
Upside/Risk	3		(3)	27		(22)	72		(52)
Target (ND/EBITDAX = 3.0x)		43			72			87	
EBITDA Minus Target	18	15	12	66	38	17	134	62	10
Net Debt/EBITDAX	1.8x	2.0x	2.1x	1.1x	1.6x	2.2x	0.6x	1.3x	2.6x
WTI Price Deck (Full Year)	$65.50	$57.76	$51.54	$82.18	$55.91	$35.47	$88.07	$54.07	$29.92
NG Price Deck (Full Year)	$2.95	$2.63	$2.38	$3.68	$2.54	$1.66	$3.84	$2.58	$1.64

FIGURE 9-8

The following table presents the same information in more detail.

FINANCIAL MODEL (90% OF OUTCOMES)

$ MM	2019			2020			2021		
	◆ HIGH	■ BASE	● LOW	◆ HIGH	■ BASE	● LOW	◆ HIGH	■ BASE	● LOW
Revenue from Market Sales	94	82	71	215	146	92	330	197	101
Derivatives Impact	(5)	3	9	(30)	3	29	(43)	2	35
REVENUE	89	85	81	185	149	121	287	199	136
Production (BOE/d)		5,321			9,745			13,635	
LOE ($/BOE)		$4.93			$3.90			$3.57	
(-) LOE		10			14			18	
Cash G&A ($/BOE)		$3.84			$2.20			$1.65	
(-) Cash G&A		7			8			8	
(-) Prod Taxes (12% of Sales)	11	10	9	26	18	11	40	24	12
EBITDAX	61	58	55	137	110	88	221	149	98
(-) Interest Expense		4			6			6	
(-) CAPX		167			167			167	
FREE CASH FLOW	(110)	(113)	(116)	(36)	(63)	(85)	48	(24)	(76)
DEBT TO EBITDAX RATIOS (@ yr end, High/Low Cases derived from Base Case of prior year)									
Cash (Q4 18E: $0 MM)	0	0	0	0	0	0	0	0	0
Revolver (Q4 18E: $0 MM)	110	113	116	149	176	198	128	200	252
Sr Notes (Q4 18E: $0 MM)		0			0			0	
Net Debt (Q4 18E: $0 MM)	110	113	116	149	176	198	128	200	252
Net Debt/EBITDAX	1.8x	2.0x	2.1x	1.1x	1.6x	2.2x	0.6x	1.3x	2.6x
WTI Price Deck (Full Year)	$65.50	$57.76	$51.54	$82.18	$55.91	$35.47	$88.07	$4.07	$29.92
NG Price Deck (Full Year)	$2.95	$2.63	$2.38	$3.68	$2.54	$1.66	$3.84	$2.58	$1.64

FIGURE 9-9

CONVERTING REVENUE AND RISKED REVENUE INTO OTHER BUDGETARY METRICS

Revenue = volumes × price

EBITDAX = revenue less G&A, taxes, and production costs

Free cash flow = EBITDAX less interest expense and CAPX (capital expenditures)

Net debt to EBITDAX ratio = (drawn revolver funds + senior notes – cash)/EBITDAX

Depending on how you measure your firm's success, you might monitor one or more of the metrics to determine when and how much to hedge. Why is this so important? Most people won't or can't calculate how a low commodity price might impact their business. This calculation is much more difficult under duress, when prices have started to fall. PRM puts this important information at your fingertips, keeping it objective and up to date. These calculations are even more important when the relationship between price and performance is not linear. This often happens when options are used for hedging and with some budgetary metrics. To illustrate nonlinear risk, see the graph in figure 9-10. This producer can rest easy when oil is above sixty dollars because a five-dollar price move does not impact its debt/EBITDA ratio very much. However, as prices go below sixty dollars, small price changes begin to grow in importance, increasing the firm's sensitivity and vulnerability to further declines. This firm should hedge aggressively at any sign of price weakness below sixty dollars or risk having a substandard debt/EBITDA ratio.

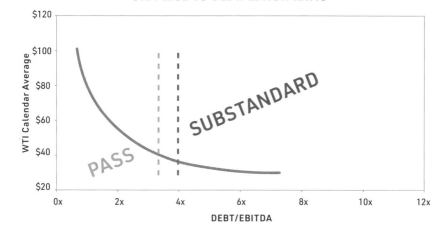

Sample company with 1MM bbl/yr production & $60MM of debt.

FIGURE 9-10

Figures 9-11 and 9-12 show how this firm's Low Case should be lifted to ensure the debt/EBITDA remains acceptable. The amount of hedging needed can be calculated by reverse engineering the math and confirmed with simulations.

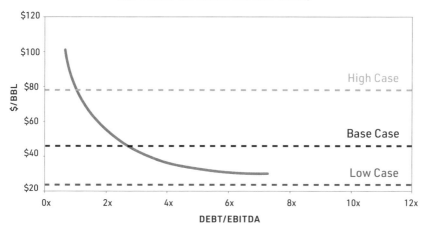

FIGURE 9-11

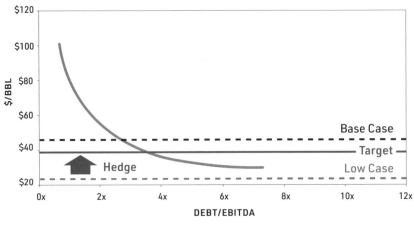

FIGURE 9-12

THE FEEDBACK LOOP

Figure 9-13 displays a series of monthly revenue observations for another company, illustrating how their revenue estimates for 2020 have changed over time. At the end of December 2018, on the left, the Base Case revenue estimate was $139 million, which was risked up to $203 million and down to $91 million. This producer had $48 million (35 percent) of the $139 million Base Case at risk. Fast-forward to June 2019 (far right)—the Base Case has climbed to $149 million + $10 million and the Low Case to $121 million + $30 million. With the passage of time and the addition of hedges (note the reduction of risk in April), risk shrank from $48 million (35 percent) to $28 million (19 percent).

2020 PERFORMANCE RISK PROFILE

	Dec-18	Jan-19	Feb-19	Mar-19	Apr-19	May-19	May-19(A)	Jun-19
Risk (%)	35%	33%	31%	29%	18%	21%	22%	19%
Risk ($ MM)	48	50	49	46	29	32	32	28
High	203	216	226	222	202	194	188	185
Base	139	150	159	160	163	151	144	149
Low	91	100	110	114	134	119	113	121

REVENUES BY PRODUCT

93%	■ Crude
4%	Nat Gas
4%	■ NGLs

RISK BY PRODUCT

90%	
1%	
9%	

2020 PRICE DECK

	WTI	NG
High	$82.18	$3.68
Base	$55.91	$2.54
Low	$35.47	$1.66

FIGURE 9-13

More detail supporting the current month's risk assessment is provided in the lower portion of Figure 9-13. This includes pie charts and the risked commodity price deck used for these calculations. On the left, the "revenues by product" pie chart shows that 93 percent of revenues will be generated from crude oil production, 4 percent from natural gas, and 4 percent from natural gas liquids (NGLs). Compare this to the "risk by product" pie chart (center). The NGLs represent 9 percent of the firm's risk, while natural gas is just 1 percent. The cause of this is that this producer hedged natural gas, probably because it is not their core product. In doing so they locked in natural gas's value but forfeited the diversification it brought to their portfolio. Natural gas hedges might have increased the firm's risk because natural gas is poorly correlated to crude oil and NGLs. Take the natural gas risk away, and you augment the risk from the other two commodities. Either exceptionally attractive gas prices or poor fundamentals may have warranted this decision, but in a vacuum this firm should have hedged their crude oil first and perhaps exclusively because that is where their risk is coming from. This can be modeled before placing hedges to verify the impact, but it is likely that as additional crude hedges are placed, NGLs will play a larger role in risk. If so, this firm should hedge more crude than they think or consider also hedging some of their NGLs.

CASE STUDY

CLIENT: Energy producer.

PROBLEM: A diversified producer of natural gas, who also produces crude oil and natural gas liquids, was focused on mitigating their risk. In the past, hedges always focused their natural gas production. By volume, they were concerned about their gas exposure. But the marketplace had changed. Oil's price, which historically traded at a ten multiple to natural gas (e.g., $20/bbl. crude and $2/MMBtu gas), was now trading near a fifty multiple. This increased the value of their oil production, both on an absolute and relative basis. R^2 was able to use data from their SEC filings to present them with a detailed analysis of their risk and where it was sourced in this new price environment.

SOLUTION: R^2 determined that after a period of rising crude oil and liquids prices, the prospective client's risk was no longer coming from gas but was now significantly generated from oil and liquids. The risk from each commodity was objectively quantified. Crude oil and natural gas liquids represented 44 percent of the prospective client's risk exposure. Now that oil was relatively more valuable, the firm's risk profile had changed.

CONCLUSION: The Board of Directors was presented with hard evidence, due to market changes, that they had become a significant oil producer. As a result, they immediately shifted gears and developed a strategy for hedging oil and NGLs.

Performing a detailed analysis of all components of the prospective client's portfolio enabled R^2 to give a clear picture of where the risk was coming from so that the risk could be managed effectively. R^2 was subsequently hired and advised on a series of hedges to bring down the risk satisfactorily to the client's defined tolerance.

HIGH-WATER MARK OF THE LOW CASE

What do you do when you don't have an obvious Hedge Target or it's no longer in reach because you missed it? In this chapter's opening example, we discussed a commodity producer who was not going to hit their budget, no matter how much they hedged, because prices were too low. In these cases, the answer is not to "do nothing and hope for the best." The prudent strategy, and often the best option, is simply to make sure your situation doesn't get any worse.

2020 PERFORMANCE RISK PROFILE

	Dec-18	Jan-19	Feb-19	Mar-19	Apr-19	May-19	May-19(A)	Jun-19
Risk (%)	35%	33%	31%	29%	18%	21%	22%	19%
Risk ($ MM)	48	50	49	46	29	32	32	28
High	203	216	226	222	202	194	188	185
Base	139	150	159	160	163	151	144	149
Low	91	100	110	114	134	119	113	121

REVENUES BY PRODUCT

93%	■ Crude	
4%	■ Nat Gas	
4%	■ NGLs	

RISK BY PRODUCT

90%
1%
9%

2020 PRICE DECK

	WTI	NG
High	$82.18	$3.68
Base	$55.91	$2.54
Low	$35.47	$1.66

FIGURE 9-14

To illustrate our point, we can see as shown in figure 9-14 that April of 2019 is the high-water mark of the Low Case. Assuming this company is going to live with the fact that they're not going to make budget and they're willing to keep that risk open for the time being, a strategy they should consider is maintaining the high-water mark of that Low Case so that once they get past April of 2019 and are in May of 2019, even though they're below budget, they are not allowing things to get any worse. The decline in that Low Case estimate can be used to trigger hedges, lifting the Low Case back to its previous high-water mark. This would allow them to defend their current position and, to the extent that they can, control how bad this year will be.

The bottom line: if the client had used PRM analysis to observe their risk profile, they probably never would have let it erode to this level! But it is never too late to begin managing your risk proactively.

Commodity producers are heavily dependent on the value of the products they sell. This is much more important when production costs are high and the margins low. Producers aren't only worried about profitability. Their shareholders and lenders often look at other budgetary metrics to track performance. Failing to identify a specific threshold for these financial targets is not a viable management strategy. Even when a specific target value is difficult to agree upon or cannot be identified, producers should consider the high-water mark of their Low Case for hedge decisions.

> **Producers should consider the high-water mark of their Low Case for hedge decisions.**

DEFENSIVE HEDGES: WHICH HEDGE THRESHOLD IS BEST FOR PRODUCERS?

In chapter 8 on consumers, we analyzed defensive hedges by compiling twelve years of pro forma WTI weighted average cost (WAC) data for six different programs (see Figure 8-21). Here we provide pro forma WTI weighted average sale prices (WASP) for producers. Again, half of these programs had a twenty-four-month hedge window and half had a twelve-month hedge window.

The table (figure 9-15) provides the weighted average sale price of WTI oil by (1) year (no hedge); (2) for each of the three various Hedge Targets; and (3) for strategies that began twelve and twenty-four months prior to the settlement window. On the far right of the table shown is the average performance achieved over the twelve years and the price difference from the "no hedge" strategy or the average settlement price of WTI.

The results are similar to those shown for consumers. Despite using six different hedge threshold calculations, in each case the average price paid did not differ in a meaningful way from the average WTI price during this period. Note that in years when settled prices were higher than in the previous year, the "no hedge" program (top row) generally resulted in the highest-priced oil (highest price is shaded in green; lowest price is shaded in yellow). When prices were lower than in the previous year, one of the hedge programs could be expected to perform best. Looking across all the producer hedge programs in oil, on average they experienced the same average result when compared to not hedging. On the surface that may not seem attractive, but neither does paying for insurance until you need it. There are two points we'd like to make here:

- The most important benefit was that budgetary objectives were achieved each year, with certainty.

- Oil prices without hedges experienced year-on-year changes that averaged $16.30/bbl. The hedge programs reduce that significantly, ranging from a low of $10/bbl. for the 50 percent of risk to a high of about $15/bbl. for the starting risk. The lower your risk threshold, the more you will hedge and will reduce volatility.

Moving on to natural gas (figure 9-16), again it is important to remember that gas prices fell by two-thirds between 2007 and 2018, from nine dollars to three dollars. Producer hedge programs are early sellers and consequently enjoy attractive hedge gains when prices fall.

Because gas prices fell with remarkable consistency, one of the hedging strategies resulted in the highest-priced gas in all but one year and on average. Simply put, the more producers hedged, the more they got paid for gas.

PRODUCER WTI

	WTI2007	WTI2008	WTI2009	WTI2010	WTI2011	WTI2012	WTI2013	WTI2014	WTI2015	WTI2016	WTI2017	WTI2018	AVG	DIFF
NO HEDGE	$72.34	$99.65	$61.80	$79.53	$95.12	$94.20	$97.97	$93.00	$48.80	$43.32	$50.95	$64.77	$75.12	
50% 12	$68.88	$82.02	$76.38	$70.16	$88.02	$90.78	$94.61	$92.67	$75.46	$52.16	$47.78	$59.24	$74.85	$(0.27)
75% 12	$70.45	$89.04	$70.50	$74.60	$92.12	$91.42	$97.01	$92.84	$69.22	$46.98	$48.82	$60.88	$75.32	$0.20
SR 12	$71.82	$96.06	$64.75	$79.03	$94.79	$92.66	$97.97	$93.00	$62.98	$42.48	$49.85	$62.60	$75.67	$0.55
50% 24	$64.98	$82.62	$62.76	$81.61	$77.68	$85.91	$91.72	$88.97	$70.35	$70.43	$59.55	$55.07	$74.30	$(0.81)
75% 24	$69.56	$89.97	$61.47	$78.96	$85.57	$90.29	$93.96	$91.52	$60.72	$64.10	$56.18	$58.67	$75.08	$(0.04)
SR 24	$72.34	$96.71	$59.91	$76.36	$92.34	$94.02	$96.52	$93.00	$51.99	$57.81	$52.81	$62.05	$75.49	$0.37

■ = highest average that year   ▨ = lowest average that year

FIGURE 9-15

PRODUCER NG

	NG2007	NG2008	NG2009	NG2010	NG2011	NG2012	NG2013	NG2014	NG2015	NG2016	NG2017	NG2018	AVG	DIFF
NO HEDGE	$6.86	$9.03	$3.99	$4.39	$4.04	$2.79	$3.65	$4.41	$2.66	$2.46	$3.11	$3.09	$4.21	
50% 12	$8.35	$8.74	$6.37	$6.29	$5.24	$4.02	$3.94	$4.26	$3.30	$3.00	$2.90	$3.10	$4.96	$0.75
75% 12	$7.87	$8.88	$5.48	$5.63	$4.67	$3.52	$3.80	$4.34	$3.02	$2.78	$2.97	$3.09	$4.67	$0.46
SR 12	$7.40	$8.99	$4.61	$4.96	$4.11	$3.03	$3.66	$4.41	$2.76	$2.57	$3.03	$3.08	$4.39	$0.18
50% 24	$6.04	$8.70	$6.06	$6.64	$6.29	$4.91	$4.56	$4.64	$3.48	$3.49	$3.39	$2.96	$5.10	$0.89
75% 24	$6.32	$8.88	$5.07	$5.84	$5.52	$4.03	$4.17	$4.48	$3.10	$3.18	$3.23	$3.00	$4.73	$0.53
SR 24	$6.62	$9.01	$4.10	$5.05	$4.76	$3.15	$3.78	$4.32	$2.72	$2.86	$3.07	$3.04	$4.37	$0.17

■ = highest average that year   ▨ = lowest average that year

FIGURE 9-16

The results in oil are similar to those shown for consumers. In gas, producers benefited where consumers didn't. And again, you may wonder, "How did R^2's clients generate the gains they did if the pro forma analysis is expected to and breaks even?" The pro forma results shown do not allow for Market Driven hedges. Like consumer hedge programs, producers will use their separate criteria to optimize defensive hedge timing and place Market Driven hedges. The evidence shows that the choice to add and the success of Market Driven hedges are largely responsible for the hedge gains our clients achieved. Our clients are the orchestrators of these decisions and deserve full credit for their success. PRM played a key role by identifying exceptional opportunities for them, but our clients made the decisions. Use the information in chapter 7 to improve the pricing of your hedge. The timing of Risk Driven hedges should be determined by your need to contain risk. Nonetheless, there is usually some window through which a statistically attractive and/or opportune moment can be identified to a client's advantage. The same goes for Market Driven hedges. The hedge gains our clients have generated demonstrate how important this can be.

Chapter Assets

- Producers use financial metrics for their Hedge Targets.
- Begin by risking revenues for the portfolio of assets and then convert these into budgetary estimates.
- Lacking a budgetary target, producers can hedge to the high-water mark of their Low Case.
- Lower risk tolerance leads to increased hedging, which results in reduced volatility but is not expected to impact the average price over time.

CHAPTER TEN

Midstream Hedging

The principle of yin and yang is that all things exist
as inseparable and contradictory opposites.

IN CHAPTER 8, we discussed consumer hedging. Consumers are the downstream portion of the value chain, where end users buy the commodity as part of the cost of delivering their services. In chapter 9, we discussed producer hedging. Producers are the upstream element of the value chain, where raw commodities are grown or pulled out of the ground. Typically, there is a midstream transport and/or processing intermediary that adds value in the chain by taking upstream materials, processing them, and delivering these processed goods to the downstream consumer.

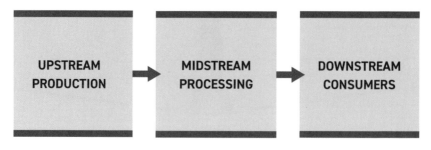

FIGURE 10-1

Note in figure 10-1 that the producers and consumers each have one arrow. That single arrow represents the risk they need to manage. It is the commodity price(s) that drives their success. The price at which producers sell and consumers buy will determine their respective success or failure. Processors, on the other hand, have two arrows—one representing the cost of supply and one representing what they sell their product(s) for. For them it is not the absolute price that matters, but the magnitude of the difference between the price of supply they buy and the price of processed/manufactured product they sell. While margins may demonstrate a pattern of improving with higher prices and eroding with lower prices, managing margins is the key to their success. One advantage that processors have is that if margins fall below zero, hedges can be cashed out and they can cease operations until it is profitable to do so. No processor will operate at negative margins willingly. In fact, while the hedges were needed when margins were attractive, they are not needed when margins are unprofitable. In such a moment, processors should monetize hedge profits, shut the facility down, and wait for better days when margins recover.

Examples of midstream processors include the following:

- Soybean processors. These operators "crush" (upstream) soybeans and sell (downstream) soybean oil (vegetable oil) and soybean meal (tofu).

- Biofuels processors. Agricultural products are turned into feeds and fuels such as ethanol and biodiesel.

- Oil refineries. These specialists turn crude oil into gasoline, diesel, jet fuel, and other products such as asphalt for roads.

- NGL fractionation. Wet natural gas is separated into components of dry natural gas, ethane, propane, butanes, natural gasoline, and condensate.

Examples of midstream operators include the following:

- Blenders. Crude oil from different locations will have different specifications that often need to be adjusted so that refineries get the grade of feedstock that they need for their unique configurations.

- Pipelines and shippers. These transporters move material from sellers to downstream buyers.

- Storage. These midstream operators provide a necessary balancing function by buying excess supply and making it available to sell when other sources of production are unavailable.

Large corporations such as Exxon have integrated upstream, midstream, and downstream operations. But globally much of the value chain is segmented, populated by many midstream players who are less capitalized and require stable cash flows.

Midstream processors (and manufacturers) should carefully manage their gross profit margins. Often these operators will have flexibility to choose which product grades they input and manage their process to generate products with attractive profit margins. Choosing the most profitable combination is optimization. While optimization enhances performance, it does not guarantee profitability.

If we model upstream inputs along with downstream outputs, we can risk the processing enterprise within known economic parameters. One complication that may surface is that a simple Monte Carlo distribution might allow a portion of the "crack spread" simulations, which represent the price of refined products minus crude oil, to go to negative values. That can happen in the real world, but it is not likely to persist for long. For example, refineries will cease operations to avoid losses. They can be expected to perform maintenance or temporarily mothball a plant before operating unprofitably. Whenever the price differential is not profitable, we can expect the collective actions of refiners to reduce the demand for crude and simultaneously limit the supply of products available. This will ultimately result in margins widening. When we allow Monte Carlo simulations to generate negative margins without economic boundaries, it is safe to assume these simulations of spread margins overestimate risk. Does that invalidate the PRM approach for a midstream entity? Absolutely not. Allow us to demonstrate why.

Refiners and manufacturers who employ PRM may overestimate the risk, but they can expect to maintain profitability. Remember: if you hedge to a target, you can expect to achieve the target.

Applying PRM to midstream firms results in an analysis that is similar to the output for the producer, where a Low Case can be managed so that risk becomes an asset. Midstream manufacturers/processors can risk their margins and hedge to protect the Low Case, just like their upstream counterparts.

TWO BITES OUT OF THE SAME APPLE

A midstream firm can hedge to raise their Low Case, just like a producer. But there are certain intrinsic advantages to midstream hedging. Generally, an upstream producer will not shut production down when it is uneconomical. Hedges should have protected their cash flow. But even when the hedges are inadequate, producers will probably need the cash flow, fear damaging the well, or have lease "held by production" clauses that make it necessary to continue operating. But when processing margins become unprofitable, some midstream firms can shut operations. Their hedges can be unwound, and with the plant shut down, the hedge gains would no longer be encumbered by processing losses, increasing profitability to the processor. Equally important, this would give the operator a second chance for profitability. Should margins return to profitable levels, new hedges can be placed and the plant restarted. This opportunity is unique to midstream operators and is another way to turn risk into an asset.

As an example, let's say that a midstream processor refines oil into gasoline. Their Base Case or current gross margin may be five cents per gallon. Let's also agree that the refining margin is risked

> Midstream manufacturers/processors can risk their margins and hedge to protect the Low Case, just like their upstream counterparts.

down two cents per gallon to three cents per gallon, which is this firm's Hedge Target. This firm needs three cents per gallon to be profitable and will hedge as necessary to protect that level (i.e., maintaining their Low Case above level). If margins widen, they do not need to add hedges. But if margins begin to erode, the refiner will hedge incrementally in a series of transactions to defend the three-cents-per-gallon Hedge Target.

Now, if gasoline prices continue to fall (or oil prices rally, or a combination of both), causing margins to narrow further, there may be a point where margins fall below three cents, which would force the refinery to operate at a loss (except for the hedges). The hedges would protect them, but this is the point where the refiner could consider taking back hedges and idle the plant. That would allow them to liquidate the hedges to lock in the gains and avoid processing for a loss. For example, if margins were one cent, the refiner would collect four cents from their hedges. If they operated, they would lose two cents, for a profitability of two cents. But if they did not operate, the four-cent gain from hedges would be all theirs. They could take this money, sit on the sidelines, and wait for margins to return to profitability. When they did, this processor would have an opportunity to place a new round of hedges covering the same period.

Efficient storage operators do this on a regular basis to maximize their midstream flexibility. The important point is that it all starts with managing your Low Case target. Once you ensure your business's profitability, risk becomes an asset by giving flexibility at lower margins and/or prices.

MIDSTREAM HEDGE STRATEGY CASE STUDIES

CASE STUDY 1

CLIENT: Midstream natural gas processor.

PROBLEM: Crude oil and natural gas were used to hedge processing margins for an NGL facility. This firm used hedges on oil to protect their NGL revenues (a.k.a. a cross commodity or proxy hedge), and senior management became concerned when the oil hedges suffered financial losses at settlement. They wondered whether these hedges might be less than effective and result in unnecessary losses. They also were not comfortable explaining losses for oil hedges when it was not one of their core products. An assessment was requested comparing pro forma results for a traditional hedge program where the NGLs would have been hedged directly using NGL swaps and collars, rather than using oil swaps as a proxy.

SOLUTION: R^2 modeled two different portfolios using direct hedges chosen by management for the comparative analysis. These strategies used financial instruments that matched the commodities, volumes, and hedge dates used in the client's portfolio. Since it was impossible to know when during the trading day the oil hedges were placed, the study compared the performance of hedge-day settlement prices rather than actual hedge prices to "normalize" the data. Historical closing price curves and volatility surfaces were used to create the pro forma results.

RESULTS: The pro forma analysis demonstrated that the hedge strategy used by the client was effective and, in fact, improved hedge returns. It was determined that on each of the hedge dates, the NGL forward curves were discounted relative to the curves for oil. These discounts would have impaired the value of the direct hedges, increasing the cost of hedging to the client by $2 million to $5 million. In addition, conventional hedges would be subject to increased slippage because the NGL market is significantly less liquid. This would have had an additional estimated cost to the client of another $1 million.

CONCLUSION: Though the selected proxy hedges were unprofitable, they were effective in providing the needed protection and outperformed the direct hedge strategies identified by management. When using proxy hedges, continuously monitoring of performance against a pro forma portfolio and the correlations between commodities is an essential part of due diligence. One cannot assume that because a strategy has worked, it will continue to work. Hedge performance reviews should be conducted quarterly. In fact, if it is observed that pricing relationships change such that oil forward prices become relatively discounted to NGLs, the firm should consider unwinding the oil hedges and replacing them with NGL hedges. Doing so under those conditions would lock in additional profits.

CASE STUDY 2

CLIENT: Midstream natural gas liquids (NGL) processor.

PROBLEM: A processor of natural gas liquids was purchasing liquids at one price location, which they transported and later sold at a different price location. The price at both locations was set by a third-party posted price. Supply and demand were important factors in determining the price at each location, which meant that the processor's profit margin was subject to market forces. The firm desired to reduce their risk, contractually fixing both the purchase and sale pricing so that incoming and outgoing prices were locked in a profit margin.

SOLUTION: R^2 reviewed the portfolio by modeling the client's prices of both the incoming stream and their outlet for the products. The portfolio was risked to determine the firm's Low Case revenue estimate. The report given to the client detailed the risk potential and quantified the risk reduction impact of incremental hedge choices within the portfolio. Assets in the portfolio were prioritized so that hedging could be undertaken in a stepwise manner.

CONCLUSION: A series of hedges was implemented, thereby reducing the risk and raising the Low Case revenue estimates to an acceptable level. Risk was reduced throughout the period so that the company could manage their contractual requirements. Hedge settlements during this period were negative, but the program was a success because the firm had hedged enough to protect budget, with no more risk mitigation than was needed. That meant the volumes it did not hedge benefitted when margins improved, generating additional profits.

CASE STUDY 3

CLIENT: Recycling processor.

PROBLEM: A refiner was able to enter into a contract to purchase used oils at a discounted price, remove impurities, and resell the refined product as a finished product (FP), referencing a more valuable, higher-quality oil price. They needed to build the plant to process the used oils, which required the commitment of capital and time. This exposed them to changing prices during the construction period. The firm desired to lock in their gross margin to ensure their return on capital.

SOLUTION: R^2 analyzed the client contracts and reviewed historical pricing data. We analyzed and determined which commodity benchmarks were highly correlated, tracking the used oil feedstock and the FP. We performed a feasibility study to assess the ability of the client to hedge feedstock and FP forward.

CONCLUSION: R^2's feasibility study concluded that the client would be able to hedge their upstream costs and downstream sales forward to lock in economic profitability. Because the Low Case identified that margins could go significantly negative, hedging most of the plant's capacity long before it was operational was advised to guarantee the plant would be profitable throughout its first three years of operation.

EPILOGUE: Once capital was committed to this project, the firm was at risk. With the signing of the construction contract, the client was exposed to changes in the gross hedge margin. Unfortunately, the client chose to not hedge. Margins collapsed during plant construction, which forced the client into foreclosure.

The moment that capital is committed to a project or investment, the margins of the business are at risk. Prior to that commitment, credit capacity for hedges must be established and a hedge strategy developed to ensure that commodity risk will be successfully managed throughout the construction period and after the project begins operations.

Chapter Assets

- Processors must manage margins—the price difference between feedstock and product.

- If margins go negative, hedges may prove to be more valuable if processing is shut in.

- Proxy hedges are sometimes necessary and can enhance profitability.

- Once capital is committed, profit margins are at risk and should be managed.

CHAPTER ELEVEN

One Process

Believe and you are halfway there

—Theodore Roosevelt

WAYNE'S FIRST BOSS, when he entered the field of risk management, loved to use what Wayne half-jokingly called a "look-back option."[3] No matter the purpose or outcome of Wayne's hedging activities, in his boss's mind Wayne was always wrong because he had either hedged too much when the hedges lost money or too little when they made money. Knowing that, Wayne found himself second-guessing every decision he had to make. As you can imagine, that was a horrible job. We caution those hedge managers employed by firms that simply hedge a percentage of risk—they, too, are exposed to "look-back options" and may eventually find themselves in a frustrating work environment … or perhaps even fired for the wrong reason.

---

3   The use of this term is casual and for illustrative purposes only. In the world of finance, there are tradable "look-back options" that are path dependent and usually priced at the optimal price over the life of the option.

When a firm adopts PRM, however, and they hedge to protect the financial targets used to measure their success, the hedges will not be measured by profitability, but effectiveness. Effectiveness is something that any good hedge manager can achieve and maintain. In this kind of culture, everyone wins—the hedge manager, the company's leadership, and the shareholders.

Effective hedging requires two ingredients: objectivity and flexibility. To achieve objectivity, human bias must be eliminated from the development of risk mitigation strategies and the tactical execution of the components used to build those strategies. Flexibility results when decisions are guided by *principles* rather than rules. Put another way, as the world changes, so will the risk/reward of your hedge strategies and the tactical implementation of the component hedges that comprise them. A principle-based organization will be flexible enough to fully benefit from all the opportunities it encounters. Here, PRM is your springboard to success. It is a universal model that distills all hedging decisions into a single process, effective across the universe of business types, commodities, and market environments. PRM will help you communicate within your organization what it needs to know to remain objective and rational in an unpredictable market environment

Think about it this way: A universal process is one where it doesn't matter if you're driving a brand new luxury car or a used economy car that has clocked so many miles that it could have gone to the moon and back—both vehicles have gas pedals, brakes, and steering wheels. Driving skill sets required to operate each are virtually identical. Further, they each have dashboards to provide you with data so that you can monitor critical factors that will help you get from point A to point B safely. Then there is your ability to adapt to changing driving conditions, which include road surface, weather, and traffic conditions. In addition, completely unpredictable events may occur while you're at the wheel, like a flat or an accident. Even though the risk factors are endless, there is only one process to driving—taking in data and making the necessary adjustments to ensure you get to where you are going safely and on time.

THE POWER OF ONE

Our experience in risk consulting for hundreds of companies over the years has found that no two businesses are alike. On the surface, one would think that consumers or producers of energy would each have risk profiles similar to their peers, and we should expect them to respond to changing market conditions at the same time, in the same way, and with the same intensity—assuming that in any moment, the "best" advice would be appropriate for all. In practice, this could not be further from reality. Every company has a unique portfolio of assets, different credit profiles, and variable operating costs—leaving each with their unique tolerance for risk. Truly, the only thing they share is their exposure to the prices of the commodities they are hedging. Each company has their own mandate for success, which completely differentiates them from their peers. Whereas one company might be trying to grow, another is trying to package themselves for a sale. These contrasting profiles require each firm to develop their own hedge strategy, and each hedge decision they make will be as unique as the company making it.

To illustrate, consider two different commodity producers with the following profiles as seen in figure 11-1:

($MM)	COMPANY A	COMPANY B
EBITDA	$300	$300
Low Case EBITDA	$200	$200
Debt	$450	$200
Debt/EBITDA	1.5	0.7
Low Case Debt/EBITDA	2.3	1.0
Max Debt/EBITDA	3.0	1.0

FIGURE 11-1

Company A is much more in debt, i.e. is more levered than Company B. Observing that, our first reaction would be to think that Company A will need to be hedging more than Company B. As it turns out, this might not be the case. It could be that management and stakeholders of Company A, perhaps because it is growing, are willing to accept more risk. Company A has a max debt/EBITDA (Hedge Target) that is three times larger than Company B's. Right now, both companies have Low Case debt/EBITDA ratios that are below their max debt/EBITDA. But note how Company B's ratio is approaching 1.0x, leaving little margin for error. In contrast, Company A has more room to breathe with an allowance of 3.0x, while its Low Case estimate is comfortably at 2.3x.

Let's move one month forward, in figure 11-2, to a time where commodity prices have dropped for both companies. Lower prices resulted in a reduction in EBITDA and Low Case EBITDA.

($MM)	COMPANY A	COMPANY B
EBITDA	$270	$270
Low Case EBITDA	$180	$180
Debt	$450	$200
Debt/EBITDA	1.7	0.7
Low Case Debt/EBITDA	2.5	1.1
Max Debt/EBITDA	3.0	1.0

FIGURE 11-2

Company A's Low Case debt/EBITDA is still comfortably below their max debt/EBITDA, so no hedging is required. Yet the less-levered Company B's Low Case debt/EBITDA (1.1X) has now exceeded its max debt/EBITDA (1.0x) ratio. If they are adhering to Process Risk Management guidelines, Company B will identify how to hedge enough of their production to raise their Low Case EBITDA from $180 million back to $200 million and implement that plan.

($MM)	COMPANY A	COMPANY B
PORTFOLIO	SAME	SAME
LEVERAGE	HIGHER	LOWER
RISK TOLERANCE	GREATER	LOWER

FIGURE 11-3

We can see from this example that one size does not fit all. Company A and Company B have the same production, EBITDA, and Low Case–risked EBITDA. Company A has more debt. Yet it is Company B that has defined *success* more conservatively, resulting in less risk tolerance. Strategically, Company B needs to respond and hedge more quickly should prices drop.

There may be any number of reasons why this is the case. Perhaps Company B is a master limited partnership that needs to distribute a much higher portion of EBITDA in dividends. Thereby, Company B's risk tolerance would be lower, and we can expect its management to be hedging a lot sooner if prices decline. The bottom line for both companies is that PRM gives them the information needed to maintain risk within tolerance and manage their enterprise successfully.

There are myriad different variables that determine a firm's success metrics and risk tolerance. Thus, there are an infinite range of risk profiles, risk tolerances, and resulting hedge solutions for businesses with commodity exposure—even for peer group companies competing in the same business. Provided that a company has clearly identified their success metrics, they can manage risk to achieve these goals.

When we are discussing process, one size fits *one*. While PRM is universally applied, each solution is unique. Using PRM allows every business to manage risk specifically as it pertains to them, accounting for the firm's unique set of assets, credit capacity, and market conditions. With PRM they can maintain risk within tolerance. Hedging to ensure budgetary success allows firms to manage risk to their enterprise's Hedge Targets, rather than trying to outguess the markets.

RULES VERSUS PRINCIPLES

One of the rules all drivers follow is to stop at red lights and wait until they turn green before proceeding. But is that wise to do under all possible circumstances? What if there was a raging wildfire sweeping across a nearby forest, as there can be in California, and it was headed right for you at an intersection where you were waiting for the light to change? In this instance, chances are you'd have a better chance of survival if you did *not* follow the rule. Instead of following the rule, you're going to apply the *principle* of driving safely and get out of there by running the red light to put as much distance between you and the fire as quickly as possible.

In the end, rules are built to fail, but principles are a framework for lasting success.

What are the basic differences between rules and principles?

PRINCIPLE: A general truth or tenet that focuses on goals to drive decisions and actions.

RULE: A regulation that includes a threat of punishment if not followed explicitly.

Hedging 50 percent of a company's volume is a rule ... and we have shown how that will eventually break down. PRM, on the other hand, is *principle driven* and supports hedging to a financial metric, allowing a firm to adjust their behavior to fit the external circumstances and/or internal changes that impact that firm's success. PRM drives adjustments that are specific to the individual company and ensures that firm's success throughout a much wider set of circumstances, because rarely are decisions black and white ... or to invoke our driving metaphor, red and green. Hedging by a percentage is a rule. Hedging by a process is a principle.

Referring to the example used earlier, a 50 percent hedge is like walking rather than running in a darkened room. You'll still bump into the wall—it might take longer to do so, and you'll be going slower, but you will hit the wall because it remains unavoidable. PRM offers you a lifeline to success. It allows you to avoid the wall by providing a stick that will warn you *before* you hit the wall. You will use this warning to protect yourself. More importantly, PRM is not just a stick that will allow you to sense the wall before you hit it; it is a smart stick designed to meet your specific requirements and adjust for market conditions.

Everyone knows what to do when they see a red light or a green light. Green means go. Red means stop. But what should a driver approaching a yellow light do? Ask a hundred drivers and you'll get a host of different answers as they consider "how yellow the light is." Some may suggest that the driver speed up. Others may say he should slow down. Either of these decisions might be the best decision for that driver in that moment. Relative factors would include the following: What is the weather like? What's the car's speed, and where is it in relation to the intersection? To get back to business, most businesses find that their margins are made or broken when the light is yellow.

PRM is the tool that enables successful execution of and adherence to hedge risk-management principles no matter what the markets throw at you.

REMOVING HUMAN BIASES

The field of behavioral economics studies cognitive bias—how people are hardwired in ways that lead many to instinctually make poor choices. Leaders in this field believe that humans, as a species, have brains that are not designed to make numerically or statistically correct choices. Human nature causes us to overvalue the importance of the newest information and undervalue the importance of older information. We speak and think about probability as a vague concept. For example, if you were to ask a group of people to define what a "good chance" of something happening is, you'll get probabilities ranging anywhere from 15 percent to 90 percent.

The book *Thinking Fast and Slow* by Danny Kahneman perfectly illustrates this point, as seen in figure 11-4.

Actual Probability	0%	1%	2%	5%	10%	20%	50%	80%	90%	95%	98%	99%	100%
Perceived Weighting	0%	6%	8%	13%	19%	26%	42%	60%	71%	79%	87%	91%	100%

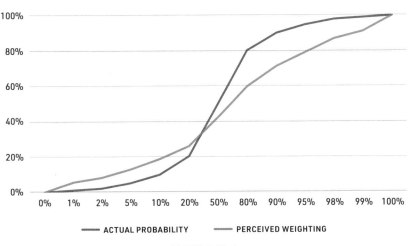

PERCEIVED WEIGHTING VS ACTUAL PROBABILITY

FIGURE 11-4

People have a perceived assessment of outcomes (orange) that weigh small likelihoods higher than actual probabilities (blue). By default, they then also weigh great likelihoods lower than actual probabilities. Consider how this impacts the way many firms hedge. Without a hedge process and left to their own devices, consumers and producers tend to be overly confident about future prices. The result is that they generally overhedge when risks are small but will underhedge when risks are great. To avoid this, many firms have opted for a hedge program that commits to a fixed percentage. But this breaks down when prices become threatening and probabilities of failure rise. At these moments, management teams will often hesitate and remain underhedged when it matters most.

To help you appreciate how this happens, consider that for an actual probability of 80–90 percent, people typically weight the likelihood of those outcomes at 60–70 percent, or a full *20 percent less* than what will take place.

This helps us to understand why a business would arbitrarily have a 50 percent hedge program. If you don't know probability and are trying to factor out human bias, hedging 50 percent means you can only be half wrong. The problem is that when more hedges are needed, when the risk increases beyond tolerance, firms are unlikely to add the additional hedges they need because they have a fully implemented hedge program. They sit there and hope because they haven't measured risk or estimated the true impact it might have on their business. Research has proven that without a process, management will continue to underestimate their risk by as much as ~20 percent below its true probability.

Essentially, Kahneman and Tversky have explained behaviorally what we as advisers see empirically—the reluctance of managers to add hedges until it is too late. In fact, managers often do not face the brutal facts until the chances of failure are approaching 100 percent. Process Risk Management, however, provides a foundation to maintain the discipline to hedge during the times when human behavioral biases would otherwise cause management to underestimate the actual risk.

> **STRATEGIC:** Identifying and monitoring the specific goals the firm wants to achieve to determine if and when hedging is appropriate.
>
> **TACTICAL:** Providing guidelines on which instruments to use, the quantity needed for that instrument and how to implement the hedge.

Based on the cognitive research, over long periods of time, PRM is an effective process that outperforms what we as humans will do if left to our own devices.

REMOVING THE "LOOK-BACK OPTION"

When management provides employees with specific and achievable goals, they are empowered to do their job. The likely result is that the employee will both perform as expected and enjoy their work. While past performance is not an indication of future outcomes, it has been our experience at R^2 that almost every one of the firms using PRM for three or more years has a profitable hedge program—profits that currently are approaching $10 billion. While past performance is no indication of future results, these clients have a consistent process for executing strategic plans and making tactical decisions.

We always caution new clients that the hedge gains or losses they will generate next year are largely influenced by randomness. Then we point out that once they have used PRM for three or more years, the influence of randomness on performance is diminished and— win, lose, or draw—the results are theirs, reflecting how well they designed their strategic plan and used our tactical tools to implement it. Three years is a short time but should provide an adequate sample.

PRM is a process-based approach that effectively eliminates the "look-back option." Once management defines Hedge Targets, you are on the road to success, provided you execute the process faithfully.

——— PRM Strategic Assets ———

- Ensures minimum metrics of success with managed hedge targets
- Gives lenders more confidence, resulting in lowering borrowing costs
- Attracts better equity valuation from the investment community
- Reduces operational risk, attracting and retaining talented employees
- Improves bottom-line performance by avoiding emotional hedges placed at inconsistent/inopportune moments
- Strengthens the company in a downturn versus peers, enabling it to opportunistically grow during otherwise difficult price environments
- Provides more opportunities to hedge at better prices because overhedging is avoided
- Expands development opportunities because cash flows are more predictable

Turning Risk into an Asset and Uncertainty into a Strategic Advantage

You can't defend the Base Case, but you can
always defend the risked case.

—Wayne Penello and Andrew Furman

HEDGING BECOMES AN ASSET when commodity price risk is managed to achieve the budgetary targets that define success. Process Risk Management is a consistent process that measures risk using these same financial metrics. It defines and monitors the likelihood of achieving the minimum levels of performance required for the firm to achieve success. PRM provides management with their own personal risk map. This map quantifies risk in budgetary terms and provides clarity to management that supports their strategic decision processes. In turn, they will often use this information to build consensus for their strategic efforts to ensure the success of their business operations.

When revenue and/or supply costs expose firms to significant commodity price risk, historically businesses have either ignored or, at best, managed the risk by using a fixed hedge percentage. During periods of rising prices for consumers or falling prices for producers, this practice often proves insufficient in meeting the needs of the business and forces management to react at inopportune moments. Their problem is, "How do we maintain the hedges needed for the proper amount of risk reduction so the firm is not over- or underhedged?" The solution: Process Risk Management. The precise and relevant nature of the information PRM provides means that hedges are "right sized," not too large or too small. This allows management teams to retain as much risk (upside) as they can afford or choose to keep. When the market provides an exceptional pricing opportunity, management is in a position to recognize its value and seize the moment to enhance performance.

How much is too much or too little? If a friend tells you they are in a car driving 45 mph, is that too slow, too fast, or just right? There is no way to assess the appropriateness of the speed of the car without a reference to surrounding conditions.

With hedge percentages, there is similarly not enough information to know if you are overhedged, underhedged, or hedged appropriately. We can take it for granted that we are driving at the appropriate speed because of driver experience and the expectation that all conditions are being factored into the decision. But we can't make similar assumptions about a volumetric hedge program that ignores many of the factors relevant to the success of the business. Now that we have learned that there is a way to identify the appropriate amount of hedging needed, why guess? Process Risk Management enables the commodity consumer, producer, or processor to hedge when, what, how, and how much is appropriate for them. It takes into consideration each of the metrics management uses to measure and communicate the success to their enterprise.

We have seen more people with mediocre ideas or talents succeed simply because they never gave up. Be persistent! What is easily overlooked, something we overlooked for a long time, is that you don't get to be persistent unless you can stay in the game. You must be a survivor. Protecting the business from irreparable harm means developing strategies that turn risk into an asset. This will support the growth of your business, enabling shareholders, employees, and their families to participate in the success. When employees are confident that your firm is a survivor, you can attract better talent, because they will be convinced that investing several years of their career in your business is likely to generate meaningful returns for them and their families. You are more likely to and can more easily raise capital, because investors and lenders will have more confidence of a successful relationship with you. Management can focus more energy on their core business because they won't have to worry about poor performance. More importantly, when peer companies are struggling, yours will be thriving. This will put you in a position to acquire new assets at fire-sale prices.

We hope you will take the experience and knowledge we have shared to grow a thriving business. Your employees and their families are assets that are leveraged every day that your risk is managed properly.

Navigating Another "Perfect Storm"

The fishermen know that the sea is dangerous and the storm terrible, but they have never found these dangers sufficient reason for remaining ashore.

—Vincent Van Gogh

EARLY IN 2020, just as we were finalizing this book, oil prices experienced another historic collapse. At one point oil prices fell 70 percent from their recent highs. The cause for this once-in-a-lifetime collapse, which in oil seems to occur every six to twelve years, was complicated. As you read this, you will likely remember that the world was paralyzed by the threat of the coronavirus pandemic, which shut down schools, businesses, and governments around the globe. Whole cities were placed on quarantine and locked down. People stayed at home. They had no reason to drive. Travel between many countries was banned. Airlines grounded airplanes and laid off thousands of employees. Demand for oil shrank by an estimated twenty-five million barrels per day, storage levels exploded, and prices imploded. WTI oil fell from $66/bbl. to $20/bbl. in what seemed like just a matter of days. But was there time for oil producers to observe and prepare for this threat before it became a reality? Yes.

Like *The Perfect Storm* in Sebastian Junger's nonfiction book of the same name, rarely is a commodity price move of this magnitude the result of a single event. This price collapse was no different. In the fall of the preceding year, oil prices were lifted by two events. In early September the Saudi Aramco refinery was bombed by drones, shutting down almost six million barrels per day or about 6 percent of the global supply. Initial reports suggested that it would be months before that plant was fully operational. Oil prices momentarily spiked to $63/bbl. on this news. Fortunately, those doomsday predictions were wrong, and the Aramco facility returned to 50 percent capacity within a week and fully operational within a month.

Then in December Saudi Aramco held the world's largest IPO, worth almost $2 trillion. The success of this IPO was dependent upon high oil prices. To ensure that the offering went smoothly, the Saudis successfully convinced other OPEC countries and Russia to reduce production. This cooperative effort kept oil prices in a $52/bbl. to $63/bbl. range, averaging over $57/bbl.

Oil prices remained strong after the IPO and peaked at $66/bbl. on January 8, 2020, when General Qasem Soleimani of the Islamic Revolutionary Guards was assassinated by an American drone. The initial spike was driven by fear that this would lead to an escalation of tension between the US and Iran. But these concerns were quickly assuaged when Iran made it clear they were not interested in a deeper conflict. That was the moment when oil prices, which had been propped up for five months, began to fall.

WEEKLY WTI PRICES
AS OF 03/13/2020

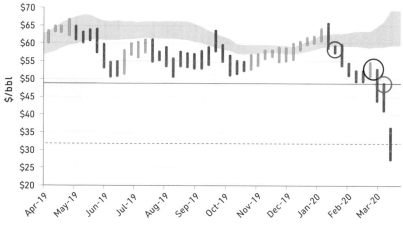

FIGURE 12-1

The weekly bar chart shows that oil prices had largely traded in the $52/bbl. to $63/bbl. range until Soleimani's assassination caused them to peak in early January. Shortly after the Iranian response, R^2 alerted its clients to the possibility that a major top was likely in place.

1/13/2020: ($58.08/bbl.) The trend reversed to DOWN. "Failure to exceed the Control Pivot of $62.16/bbl. this week is evidence that a major top is in place." (Pivot was not exceeded; see the purple circle above.)

Reason for concern was elevated because in the previous week, the oil price Trend turned to DOWN and sellers took Control of the market. This is rarely a good sign for producers, but at least this was happening when spot oil prices were trading near $59/bbl. While evidence mounted that a top was in place, prices remained strong. This was a good time for producers to consider Market-Driven hedges. During the ensuing months, prices continued to fall. Among the several warnings we issued was this:

2/3/2020: ($50.11/bbl.) "Despite the sharp selloff, R^2 is concerned that prices can go lower and strongly recommends hedging to protect minimum Revenue/Cash Flow metrics. Consider waiting to hedge (1) when spot rallies to the Control Pivot ($52.67/bbl.), or (2) when renewed weakness is indicated with prices falling below the prior week low ($50.97/bbl.)." (Both prices were achieved; see black circle above.)

Regardless of our warnings, clients who used PRM to monitor their Low Case risked estimates could see how lower prices were having a negative impact on their businesses. They knew the magnitude of the impact and had time to add hedges to their portfolios to protect themselves. By the end of February our risk curves for oil were allowing for a drop below $30/bbl. Up to this point spot prices worked their way down from a momentary peak at $66/bbl. to about $50/bbl., about a 25 percent decline. This decline was significant but pales in comparison to the $30/bbl. drop that followed. Then we wrote the following:

3/2/2020: ($46.75/bbl.) "R^2 has concerns that prices can continue lower due to greater macro recession likelihood, and strongly recommends hedging to protect minimum Revenue/Cash Flow metrics. This month we recommend adding Defensive Hedges between Friday's high of $47.03/bbl. and this week's Control Pivot of $48.25/bbl." (Prices rallied to $48.66/bbl. before collapsing; see blue circle above)

Just thirteen trading days later, oil prices fell to $20/bbl. Clearly producers had an early opportunity to add Market-Driven hedges to take advantage of attractive prices and then two months to proactively add Risk-Driven hedges to protect their Low Case benchmark(s). By the end of February, producers who used PRM to manage their risk, and protect their Low Case Target(s), already had sizable hedges in place. Just a small fraction of their business was exposed to the drop that was about to happen. In most of these cases, when barrels were not protected with hedges, clients had a strategic plan in place to manage the risk operationally; that is, capital that would not be spent and wells that would not be drilled or could be shut in.

During the first quarter of 2020, R^2 clients had hedge portfolios that generated $10 *billion* from cash settlements and market gains on open hedge positions. Some of the gains were on hedges in 2021 and 2022. For those clients who needed additional cash flow in 2020, these hedges were a resource that could be restructured or liquidated to bring that value forward and help them to survive until prices recovered.

Anyone can appear to be a good sailor when the seas are calm. It's how one handles the storms that separates the great sailors from others in the fleet. While the timing of storms may be impossible to predict, their magnitude is not. Good sailors are prepared for and keep an active look out for storms. The data in Figure 9-3 of this book was published at the end of August in 2019. At that time Cal 2020 swaps were trading $52.17 (Base Case) and the Low Case estimate for these swaps was risked down to $33.22. Unfortunately for producers, less than a year later this Low Case estimate became a reality, i.e. the new Base Case. In the months that follow this price downturn, we will certainly learn of oil companies that were capsized by this storm. Of the survivors, some were lucky, but we advise many that took this early assessment and subsequent warnings seriously. They were prepared for and successfully navigated this storm's turbulent waters. These firms illustrate perfectly that, even under extreme market conditions, by employing Process Risk Management, "risk is an asset."

ABOUT R^2

Since its inception in 2001 by Wayne Penello, R^2 has built a reputation for its expertise as an independent, full-service adviser that works with clients to build hedge programs that protect value and accelerate growth. The R^2 team includes nine professionals with a variety of backgrounds in trading, finance, and quantitative disciplines.

PHILOSOPHY

The keys to a successful hedge program are objectivity, quantification, and consistency. We quantify risk using the same financial metrics that our clients use to measure their success. This allows them to proactively hedge and to align those hedges to specific financial goals.

R^2's patented analytics are presented in budgetary terms to help clients fully appreciate market risks and opportunities. This results in hedge portfolios that ensure budgetary success and have generated almost $10 billion in hedge receivables.

INFRASTRUCTURE

R^2 assists clients with the various aspects of establishing a hedge program: hedge policy document review, ISDA assistance, Dodd-Frank compliance, counterparty credit introductions, and risk assessments.

SYSTEMS AND DATA

Deal information is held in secure databases with audit trail capability. Through R^2's online portal, Drill, clients have access to their hedge portfolio, market valuations, various forward curves and volatility surfaces.

TRANSACTIONAL SUPPORT

Our pricing desk has the experience, tools, and relationships needed to successfully negotiate with counterparties and minimize transaction costs.

VALUATIONS AND REPORTING

R^2's reports are SSAE 18/SOC compliant. More than fifty firms use R^2 for hedge portfolio valuations.

MARKET INSIGHT

Monthly, weekly, and special reports inform clients on commodity fundamentals, price signals, and our views on price direction.

RISK ANALYTICS AND HEDGE ADVISORY

R^2 provides clients with thorough and timely information about their risk profile and specific hedge recommendations to achieve bottom-line goals.

—————— CONTACT ——————

Wayne Penello
wpenello@riskedrevenue.com

Andrew Furman
afurman@riskedrevenue.com

Risked Revenue Energy Associates (R^2)
2323 South Shepherd Drive, Suite 1011
Houston, TX 77019
(713) 522-6161